THE MONSTER BOOK OF LOGIC PUZZLES & SUDOKU

nikoli

PUZZLE WRIGHT PRESS

An imprint of Sterling
Publishing Co., Inc.
www.puzzlewright.com

Puzzlewright Press and the distinctive Puzzlewright Press logo are
registered trademarks of Sterling Publishing Co., Inc.

2   4   6   8   10   9   7   5   3   1

The puzzles in this volume were excerpted from *Akari & Sudoku, Fillomino & Sudoku,
Hashi & Sudoku, Heyawake & Sudoku, Hitori & Sudoku, LITS & Sudoku, Masyu & Sudoku,
Number Link & Sudoku, Nurikabe & Sudoku, Ripple Effect & Sudoku, Shikaku & Sudoku,
Slitherlink & Sudoku,* and *Yajilin & Sudoku* © 2008–2010 by Nikoli

Published by Sterling Publishing Co., Inc.
387 Park Avenue South, New York, NY 10016
© 2010 by Sterling Publishing Co., Inc.
Distributed in Canada by Sterling Publishing
^c/o Canadian Manda Group, 165 Dufferin Street
Toronto, Ontario, Canada M6K 3H6
Distributed in the United Kingdom by GMC Distribution Services
Castle Place, 166 High Street, Lewes, East Sussex, England BN7 1XU
Distributed in Australia by Capricorn Link (Australia) Pty. Ltd.
P.O. Box 704, Windsor, NSW 2756, Australia

Sterling ISBN 978-1-4027-7880-3

For information about custom editions, special sales, premium and
corporate purchases, please contact Sterling Special Sales
Department at 800-805-5489 or specialsales@sterlingpublishing.com.

CONTENTS

INTRODUCTION

Welcome to *The Monster Book of Logic Puzzles & Sudoku*, which is one of the largest collections of logic puzzles ever assembled. Here you will find many different puzzle types that will stretch your mind in new ways. There are 14 puzzle types in all, for a total of 360 puzzles, and every single puzzle within these pages was handcrafted by Nikoli, a leading innovator in the field of logic-based puzzles.

The puzzles themselves are arranged alphabetically by puzzle type, except for sudoku, which appears last. The puzzles start out small and easy within each section, growing in size and difficulty as the section progresses. Be sure and read each introduction along the way, even if you think you already know how to solve that kind of puzzle, since some new techniques may be revealed. You are bound to discover other techniques on your own, but it's nice to start out with some idea of how to begin.

So what are you waiting for? Grab a sharp pencil and prepare to do battle with a monster. A *Monster Book of Logic Puzzles & Sudoku*, that is.

—Nikoli

AKARI

When solving an akari puzzle, the grid must be filled with light bulbs (represented by circles) so that every square is illuminated. When a light bulb is placed in the grid, it illuminates every square in a horizontal or vertical line that isn't blocked by a black square. However, no light bulb may be illuminated by another light bulb, and the bulbs must be placed so that each numbered has the correct number of light bulbs adjacent to it.

Let's solve an akari puzzle together so you can get used to some of the basic solving strategies. The easiest place to start is around the 4. Every square adjacent to the 4 must contain

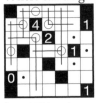

a light bulb, so we can draw in four circles right away. Having placed those light bulbs, there are now two light bulbs adjacent to the nearby 2, so we can draw dots in the other two squares next to that 2 to indicate that they must be empty. (And we can do the same in the squares next to the zero.)

Now that we've placed some light bulbs, let's look at what squares they illuminate. Remember a light bulb illuminates all squares in a horizontal or vertical line, until the beam of light is interrupted by a black square. So if we draw lines in all directions from the four light bulbs whose locations we know, we can see which squares have been lit up (and which, therefore, do not contain light bulbs, because no light bulb may be illuminated by another bulb).

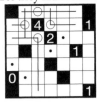

From here, we can make quite a few deductions. Take a look at that empty square in the leftmost column. Every white square in the grid needs to be illuminated. Where can a light bulb be placed to illuminate this square? Not in the square below it or in either of the two squares above it, and there's a black square to the right. This square must have a light bulb on it. Similarly, the square below the 2 is unlit. There's only one square in which a bulb can be placed to light it up, just to its right. That's the one bulb adjacent to that 1, so we can add dots around it, and draw in the lines of the new bulbs as well.

We're almost done now. There's a light bulb shining on one side of the 1 in the upper right, so the bulb adjacent to that square must be below it. That light bulb will cast a light straight down to the 1 in the lower right corner, preventing a bulb from being placed in the square above it. Therefore the bulb next to that square goes to its left. This leaves only three unlit squares, one of which has a dot in it because it's next to the zero. The only way to light all the remaining squares is to place light bulbs in the two available squares with no dot in them. And that's it!

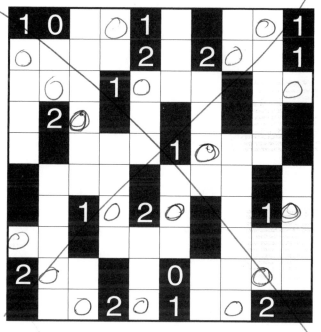

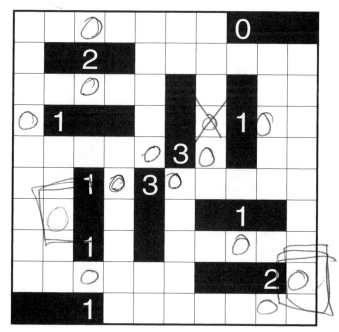

3 EASY

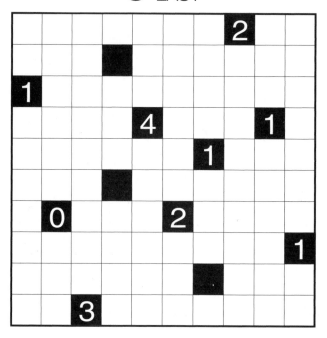

4 EASY

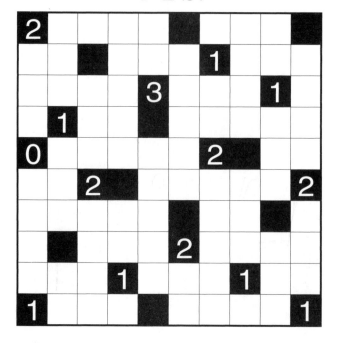

7 EASY

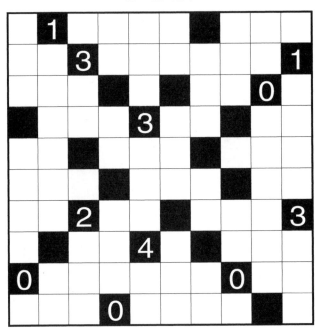

8 EASY

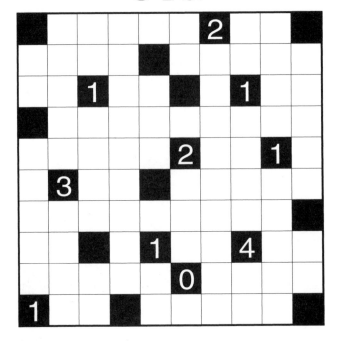

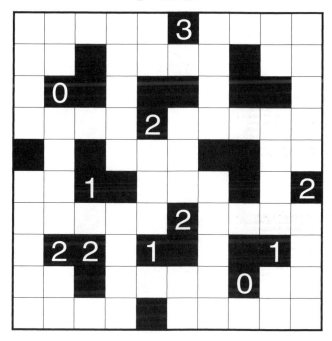

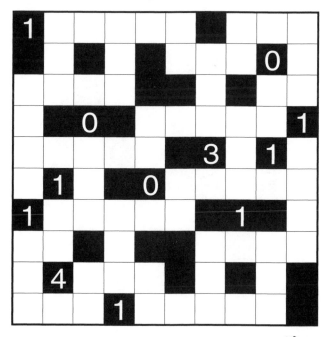

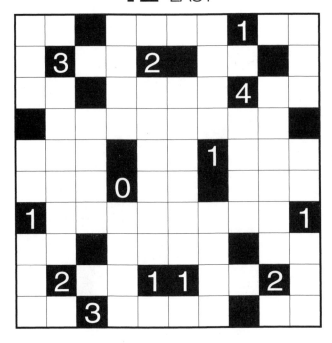

13 MEDIUM

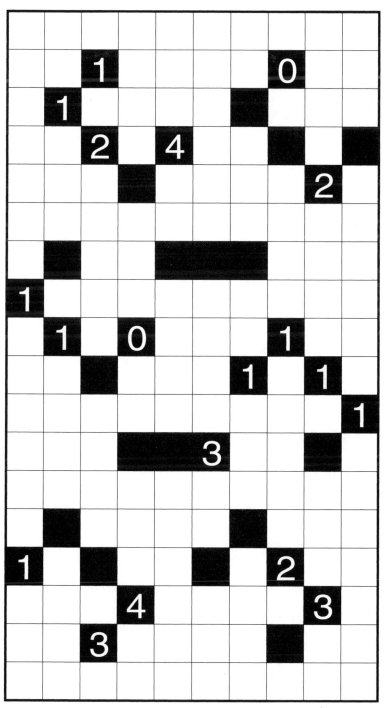

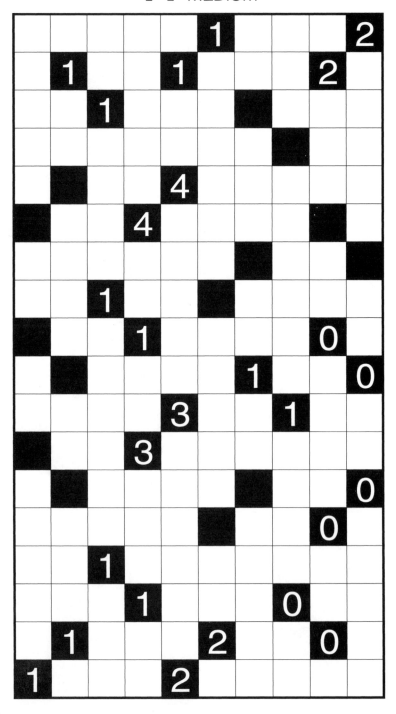

15 MEDIUM

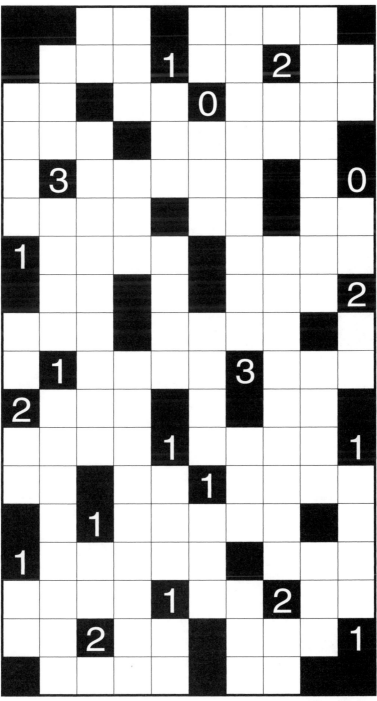

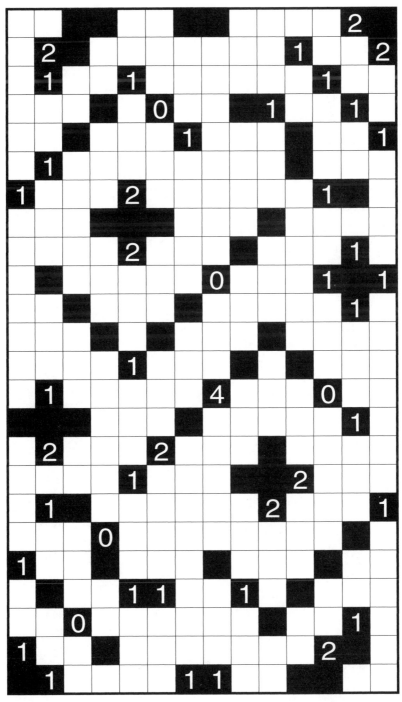

19 MEDIUM

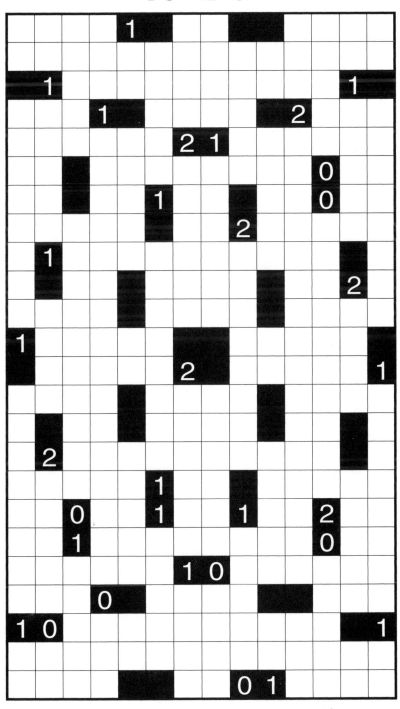

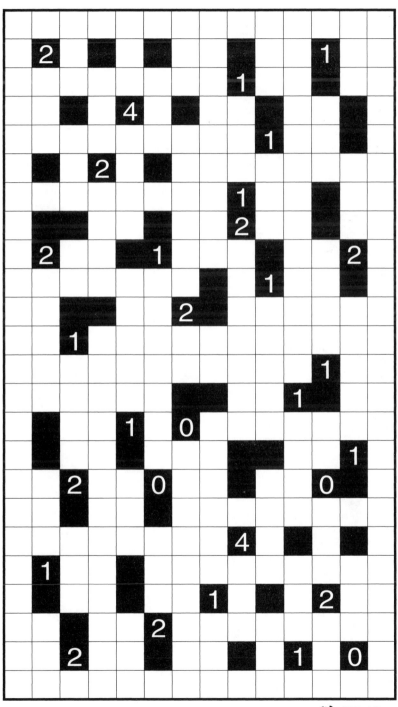

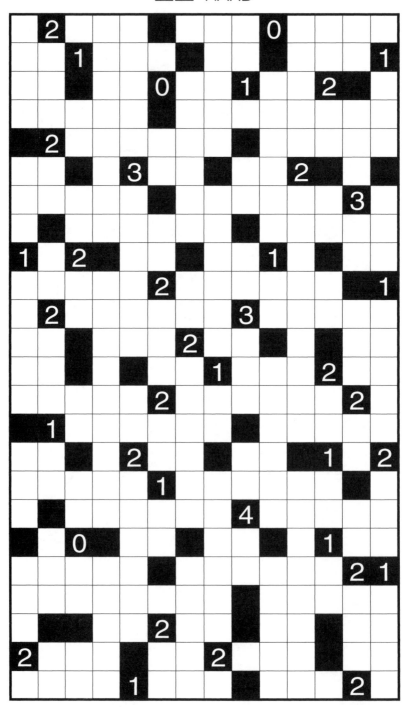

23 HARD

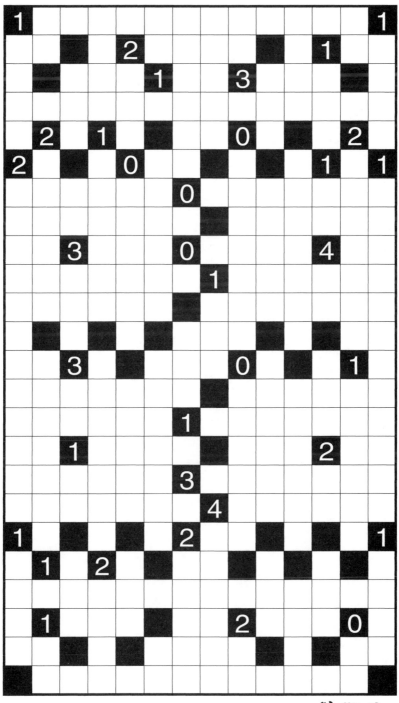

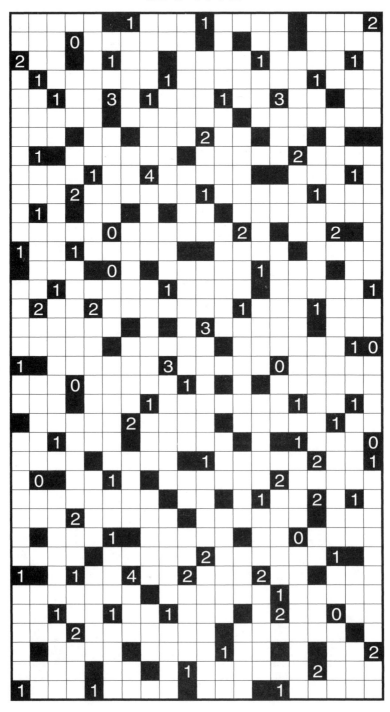

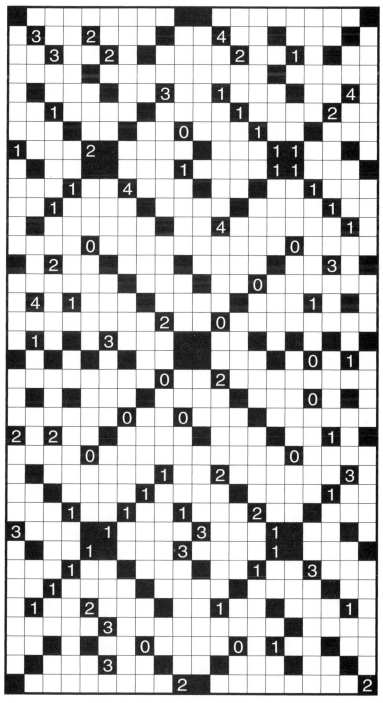

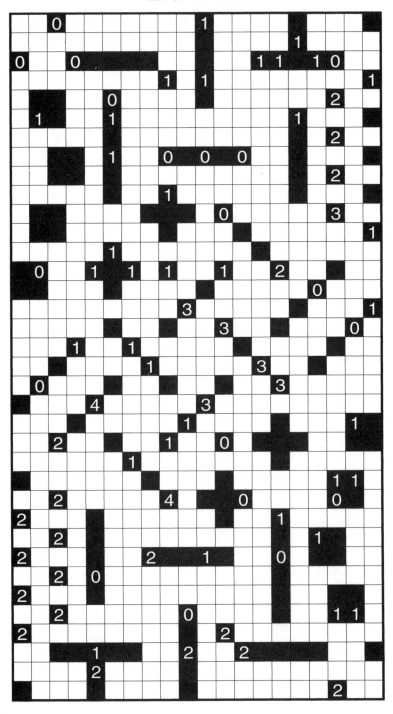

FILLOMINO

A fillomino puzzle starts out with a grid in which some numbers have been filled in. Each number is part of a block of cells (separated from other blocks by thick black lines) that contains a number of squares equal to that number. Not all blocks of cells contain numbers placed in advance, leaving you to deduce their contents. Your goal is to fill the grid with numbers so that every square is filled, and no block of cells is horizontally or vertically adjacent to another block that contains the same number.

Let's take a look at a small sample puzzle so you can see how it works. There are a few places we can start making deductions. One thing we can do is find all the given 1s in the grid and draw black lines around them, since the number 1 indicates a block of cells with only one cell in it. We can also draw black lines between any two given numbers that are horizontally or vertically adjacent but aren't identical, since they're clearly not contained within the same block. What else can we do? Take a look at those two pairs of diagonally adjacent 2s. For each pair, neither of the two squares adjacent to both 2s can contain a 2, because then there would be three connected 2s, which is impossible: a block with a 2 in it contains two connected cells, not three. Therefore those diagonally adjacent 2s are in different blocks, and we can draw black lines to close off the directions in which those blocks cannot extend. The grid now looks like this.

The 2 in the upper left corner is now completely contained inside a two-cell block, so we can write a 2 into the empty square to complete that block. Similarly, the 2 in the fifth row can only extend in one direction: to the right. That square must also contain a 2, and since that completes the block of two cells, we can surround it with dark lines. Next, let's take a look at those two connected 3s on the left side of the grid. There must be one more 3 connected to them, to make a block of three cells, but that third 3 can't be adjacent to any of the nearby 3s or there would be four connected 3s, which is impossible. So, just as we did with the 2s earlier, we can draw dark lines to block off those squares.

There's quite a bit we can do now. There's an empty cell in the lower left corner; it's a one-cell block, so we can write a 1 in it. The 3 on the bottom row must extend to the right, connecting to the nearby 3 two cells to the right. That completes a three-cell block, so we can draw a thick line around those three cells. As for the 3s on the left side of the grid, there's only one place remaining for the third 3 to go, so write that in and complete the thick border. Once that's done, the two-cell area in the lower left is completely defined, so a 2 can go in the empty cell to complete it.

Now take a look at the 4 in the top row. It must be part of a four-cell block, and there are only three more cells it can possibly extend to. Therefore the three adjacent cells all contain 4's, completing that block. In the lower right, we can use similar logic to determine where the second 2 in that corner should go. Can it extend to the left? No, because if it did, that wouldn't leave enough available cells for the nearby 4 block. It must therefore extend down into the corner.

```
2 2 |   4 |   2
1 | 2 |   6 |   6
3 |       3 |   3
            5
3 3 |   2 2 |   3
3 2 2 |   4 |   2
1 3 3 3 |   1
```

Let's go back to the left side. The remaining 3 extends to the right, but doesn't continue to the right or there would be four connected 3's. Which direction does it go from there? If it goes down, that would leave a single isolated block above it, which could only contain a 1. However, there is already a 1 block adjacent to that square, and no two blocks with identical numbers may be adjacent. Therefore the block extends upward into that square and can be surrounded by dark lines. The nearby 2 can only extend downward, completing that block, which means the adjacent 3 can only go to the right and then down.

```
2 2 4 4 4 2
1 | 2 4 6 |   6
3 |       3 |   3
            5
3 3 |   2 2 |   3
3 2 2 |   4 |   2
1 3 3 3 |   1 2
```

```
2 2 4 4 4 2
1 3 2 4 6 |   6
3 3 2 3 3 |   3
            5 3
3 3 |   2 2 |   3
3 2 2 |   4 |   2
1 3 3 3 |   1 2
```

We're getting close to done. There are four empty squares that the 5 can extend to, so we can fill those in with 5s to complete that block. The 2 in the upper right can't extend down or it would isolate the 6s in areas too small for them, so it extends to the right, and the 6s connect to each other and can begin extending downward.

```
2 2 4 4 4 2 2
1 3 2 4 6 6 6
3 3 2 3 3 6 3
5 5 5 5 3 6
3 3 5 2 2 |   3
3 2 2 |   4 |   2
1 3 3 3 |   1 2
```

You can probably take it from here, but we'll go step by step anyway. The 3 on the right must extend down, connecting to the 3 below it. This leaves only one square where the sixth 6 can go, and once that's filled in, every remaining square is part of the block of four cells with the 4 in it. Fill those in with 4s, and we're done!

You'll discover more solving techniques as you go. Although the rules of fillomino are simple, as with sudoku, those simple rules lead to many interesting strategies. Enjoy!

```
2 2 4 4 4 2 2
1 3 2 4 6 6 6
3 3 2 3 3 6 3
5 5 5 5 3 6 3
3 3 5 2 2 6 3
3 2 2 4 4 4 2
1 3 3 3 4 1 2
```

27 EASY

3	2				2				5
		3		3		3			
		2				2			
7	2			3	4			5	2
			2			3			
			5			4			
3	4			5	3			4	4
		1				2			
			3		2	3			
3			2					3	3

28 EASY

3			3			3			6
6			5			6			4
		6	2				2	6	
4			2			6			
	3			3			3		
		2			6			2	
			6			4			2
	4	2					3	3	
2			4			3			4
3			6			2			2

29 EASY

```
2 4 . | . . . | 3 5 .
. . . | . . . | 5 2 . 4 5
. 5 3 | . . . | . . 3 3
. 4 1 | . 5 1 | . . .
4 . . | . 3 3 | . . 2
3 . . | 2 1 . | . . 5
. . . | 4 7 . | 3 5 .
2 4 . | . . . | 5 3 .
6 1 . | 7 5 . | . . .
. . . | 3 3 . | . 2 6
```

30 EASY

```
. 4 3 | . . 3 1 | . .
. 3 4 | . . 3 6 | . .
. 2 4 5 | . . . | 4 3
4 2 . | . 3 2 6 | . .
. 5 2 1 | . . . | 3 3
4 3 . | . 5 2 3 | . .
. 4 2 | . . 1 2 | . .
. 3 4 | . . 3 6 | . .
```

30

31 EASY

	5	6			2				
	3								6
		6	6			3	3	4	
						6			
5		3	2	2				2	6
1	5				6	1	3		4
			2						
	5	5	5			3	5		
2								2	
				5			2	4	

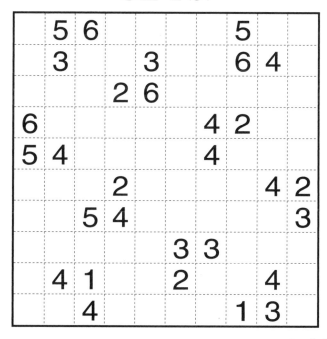

32 EASY

	5	6					5		
	3			3			6	4	
			2	6					
6						4	2		
5	4					4			
			2					4	2
		5	4						3
					3	3			
	4	1			2			4	
		4					1	3	

						5		
6	2	5	6			1	2	4
					2			
	2				5		2	3
	5		2	3			5	
	2				3	3	4	
2	1			4			2	
				4				
3	4	3				3	5	6	5
	4							

	3	4			4	2	1	
2			1	2				2
3			2	1				6
	4	2		4				3
					4	2	6	
	4	3	5					
2			3		2	3		
4			1	3			2	
4			5	1			1	
	3	5	2		5	2		

		8	2		2	9		
	5						5	
2			5	5				9
5			5	5	5	2		2
					4	3		
		4	4					
4		4	4		4	4		3
5					5	2		6
	2						1	
		4	4		4	6		

		2		1	2		7	
		3					6	
3	2	4			7	3	1	6
					4			2
	4		5			2		3
3		4			5		4	
5				1				
4	2	1		4		2	2	7
		6				6		
		1		2	3	3		

				3				
	2			4	5	4	2	
4	1	2		2				5
	5			6				5
				6	2	5		6
2		2	1	2				
5				2			6	
4				5		2	1	3
	5	2	5	2			3	
				5				

6	6			5	2			
	4						4	2
			1	6			2	3
	2	6						
3					6	4	3	4
	2	3	3	6				4
							4	3
	5	3			3	2		
	3	4						2
				2	6		3	4

4			4	2	3	2			3
	1						5		
	2							1	
3			5	6	6	5			4
	4					4			
	2			4	2			5	
3			3			4			6
	3					2			
3	3		5	1		1			5
8	4		1	5		2			2
	5					1			
2			7			4			6
	2		5	4			4		
	1					2			
3			7	1	3	2			4
	1						1		
	7					5			
4			3	6	3	4			3

4	2	4			4	3	6
5	2		4	3	2	3		5	6
		1					2
		5					5
5	3		4	5	4	4		4	3
	3	3		2	1		2	6
7			3			2			3
2			7			3			3
	7	2		7	4		4	1
4	7		7	3	4	2		6	5
		4					6
		2					5
5	2		4	7	3	6		4	4
	5	4	2			7	4	2

				6					
3	4	3		3	3	4		6	
		2						5	
7		3		3		5	2	3	
7			2						
1	2	4		3	1		5		
							3		
				4			5	3	2
3	5	5	4	5					
					6	6	2	1	6
3	1	2			3				
		3							
		2		4	3		2	3	2
					4				3
	2	3	1		2		3		4
	5						1		
	4		4	3	4		4	5	2
				5					

42 MEDIUM

2	2			5	4	
4	3			4	3	
	5	3	3		4	
5		6		5		2
2			2	5		4
5						8
	6	5	2		5	5	3
			2	4		
5		1			4	8
2		2			4	2
			5	3		
	3	4	5		7	3	4
3						4
3			5	7		3
2		4		4		2
	4		3	4	4	
	2	3		4	2	
	5	6		6	3	

38

4	5	3			3	6	3	
				2				3
			2				1	
				4				4
4	5	4			4	5	2	
				4				4
			1				4	
				1				5
4	3	6			6	1	5	
	2	4	1			2	3	5
1				4				
	2				7			
6				4				
	2	4	6			4	3	5
2				3				
	2				6			
2				1				
	4	6	1			2	4	1

		2	3	2				
		6	6	6		5	2	
						4	7	
	6	3				4	4	
	2	7						
	4	6		5	4	3		
				3	3	7		
			5	2	4			
			2	5	8		7	6
							3	1
		4	2				5	6
		5	4					
		2	3		5	4	6	
					6	3	2	

45 MEDIUM

				1			2	
		8	2		8	2		
2			4	2				5
		2		4	3		2	
	2							3
			3	2		5		
8	2		4	4				3
6			8		2		4	2
		4			2			
				4		2		
6	3		4		4			3
6					2	3	2	4
		3		3	2			
2							2	
		3		3	3		2	
2					3	3		3
		3	3			5	3	
	3			3				

	2		2		1			
	3		7		6			
	3		2		7			
	1		3		3			
	2		2		2			
5	4		6		1			
			3		3	1	2	
			2					
2	4	3	2	6				
				7	1	3	2	3
				3				
1	4	4		4				
	2			5		1	2	
	7			4		3		
	5			7		4		
	1			3		2		
	5			5		1		
	8			4		4		

4	2		1	2	5			2
						4		4
	2	4			2		3	
					3	4		4
4		4	3		3		3	
							2	1
	4	4			3			8
				2	6		3	
3	2				8			
				5			3	6
		2		1	6			
4		3		6		6	3	
1		3						
		3		5		2	3	4
2			2	3				
		4		3			4	3
3		2						
3				3	1	3		3	2

48 HARD

2	3			6		6		5
			2			2		2
		3				5		3
	5			7			3	
3								
		1	3	7				
		3		7		9	3	9
5		3	2	5		4		1
						2	4	5
	6	3	2					
	3		7		4	1	3	5
	6	4	5		7		2	
					8	2	5	
								5
		5			8		3	
	3		5				5	
	4		3			8		
	3		3		3		2	5

		3		4				3	3
		4		3			3		
4	3			2			5		
			2					2	2
3	4	4			4	3	2		
			5		3		5		
3		5		3		3			3
8			1		5		3		3
8		1		1		2			9
3			2		4		6		2
		2		2		2			
		3	3	5			4	5	2
3	4					5			
		2			5			5	2
		2			3		4		
4	4				4		7		

50 HARD

				1	3		3	3	
4	5				1	2	4		1
1	2	2	3		4		3	4	
		4	2	2	3				1
				1	2	4	2		
	1					3	5	3	5
2		5	4					2	1
	2	8	3	3	3				
3				5	1	3	4		
	8					6	1	4	4
1		3	3					1	2
	8			4	6	1	3		
		4	3		6	4		1	
6	6					1	2		4
2	5	4	1					3	
		2	3	6	5				6
				2	5	5	2	2	
4	1					6	3		6
2	3	4	3					6	
		2	5	2	5				
3				3	3	4	3		
	2	2		1		3	6	3	4
1	3		4	3				4	6
	2	2		4	3				

51 HARD

		4			5			7			7		
		5			5			4			5		
2	1		4	6		7	4		4	2		2	7
4	6			5	1			5	4			1	2
5	3		3			7	5			3		5	4
			5			7	5			5			
	3			3	5			4	4			6	
	3			4	4			7	7			2	
	4		5			3	3			6		4	
	4		6			6	6			5		1	
				5	5			6	4				
				6	4			4	5				
	4			6		4	3			6		6	
	7			3		5	3			5		3	
	3			3	3			2	1			5	
	2			4	5			1	5			4	
			6			2	5			6			
6	7		7			6	5			4		4	3
3	7			6	7			4	3			6	5
4	5		2	4		3	3		3	6		6	4
		2			4			4				4	
		5			3			2				2	

4	4		4			4		3	2	1
			3			4		4		
	6		4	3	4	4	3	3		
		4						1		
						3		4	2	4
		3	2	3	6	3	3			
		6			2					
		3			1	5	2	6	6	4
		2			5	2				6
		4	4	3	1	5	1			1
							6			6
					2	5	3	4	1	4
3	1	3	4	2		6				
5			6							
5			5		1	2	3	5	3	
4			5		2				5	
4	6	5	1	3		6			4	
						4			5	
			3		3	4	5	1	4	
4	3	3		3						
	5								2	
	5			5	3	5	2	5	2	
	5			1			5			
5	5	3		5		1			2	5

HASHI

Hashiwokakero—or "hashi" for short—is a puzzle in which a set of islands must be connected into one large network by drawing bridges horizontally and vertically between them. The number on each island indicates the number of bridges that are connected to it. Any pair of islands may have at most two bridges connecting them, and bridges may not cross each other or pass over the other islands.

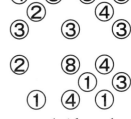

Let's take a look at an easy hashi puzzle so you can see how it works. There are a few places we could begin in this puzzle, but let's start with the island in the lower middle marked with an 8. The number means that there are eight bridges that connect to this island. Since no two islands can have more than two bridges that connect them, this means that there must be exactly two bridges

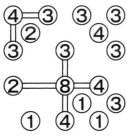

between the 8 island and the islands directly to the north, south, east, and west of it. We can do the same thing with the 4 island in the upper left corner, which has only two islands it can connect to (to the west and south), so two bridges connect to each of those islands from the 4 island.

What about the 3 island in the upper right corner? We can't place all of its bridges, but we can place some. Since it's not possible for all three bridges to go to just one of the two islands reachable from there, we know that each island must have at least one bridge, so we can draw those in. We'll place the third one later.

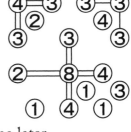

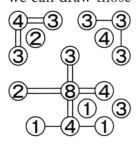

Now let's move to the lower left. That 1 island has a 2 island to its north and a 4 island to its east. There can't be a bridge between it and the island to the north, however, because there's a bridge in the way. (Two bridges, actually.) So that island's bridge extends to the east, which accounts for three of that

49

island's four bridges; the fourth one extends east to the other 1 island along the bottom of the puzzle.

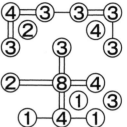

We're almost done. The first 3 island in the top row already has two bridges connected to it, and no island to its south, so the third bridge must extend east to the next 3 island. Similarly, that island also has no island to its south, so its one unaccounted-for bridge must extend east to the 3 island in the corner, completing the set of three bridges for that island. The 4 island near the upper right corner has only two islands that it can connect to, so two bridges extend to each of those islands (thus completing the connections for those islands).

Just a few bridges left. The 3 island in the lower right has one available spot for a bridge to the west (since the 1 island can only take one bridge) and two to the north (which accounts for that island's second and third bridges). That's all three bridges, so we

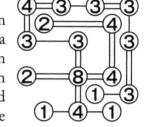

can draw those in. Right now the islands are divided up into two separate networks, and they must all be connected up into a single network for the puzzle to be solved. Fortunately the last bridge remaining (between the two 3 islands in the third row, each with one bridge unaccounted-for), connects these sets of islands up—mission accomplished!

①—① Remember to keep the rule in mind that all islands
②═② must be connected somehow. Sometimes making a connection would isolate some islands, which means you'll know that connection is impossible. (For instance, two 1 islands can never directly link to each other, since then no other islands would ever be able to reach them; no other bridges could ever connect to either island. Similarly, if two 2 islands are in a line with each other, they can be connected by at most one bridge, or they would also be unreachable by any other island.) You'll discover more solving techniques as you go. Have fun!

53 EASY

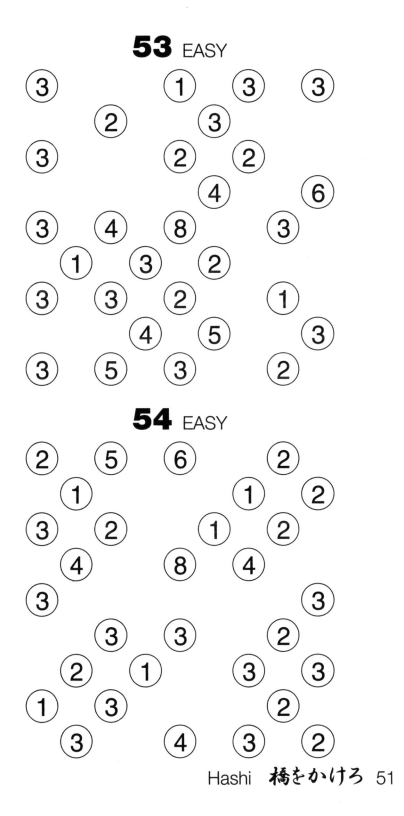

54 EASY

55 EASY

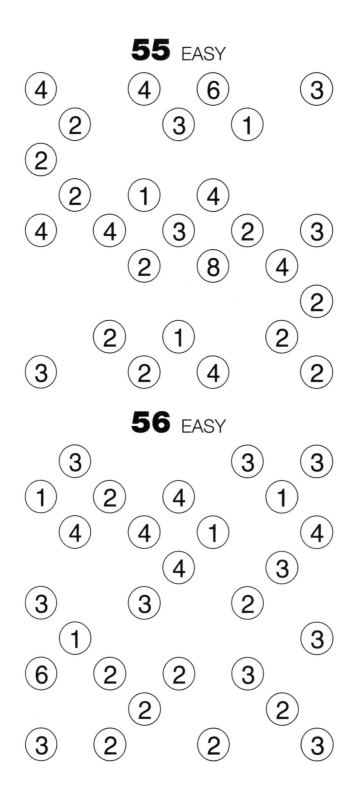

56 EASY

57 EASY

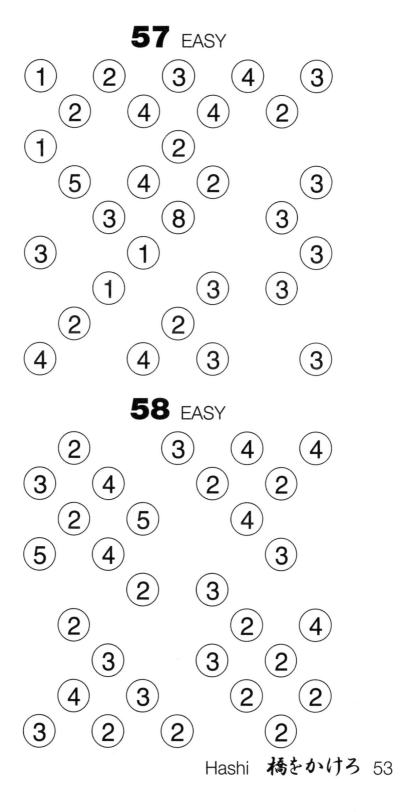

58 EASY

59 EASY

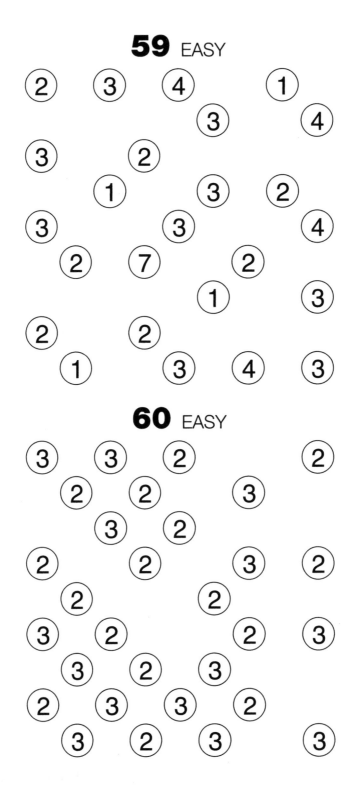

60 EASY

54

61 EASY

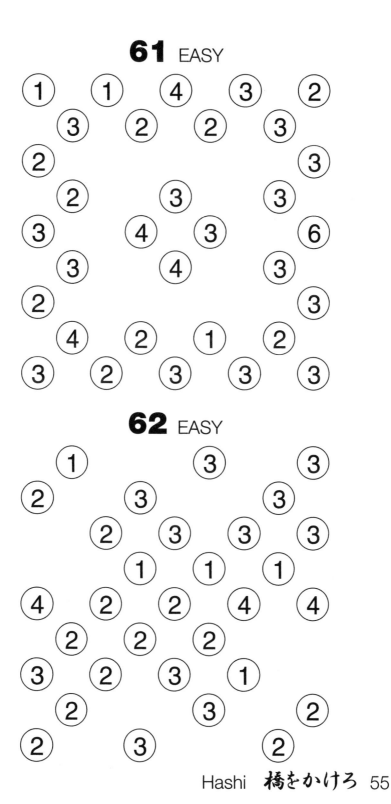

62 EASY

63 EASY

64 EASY

65 MEDIUM

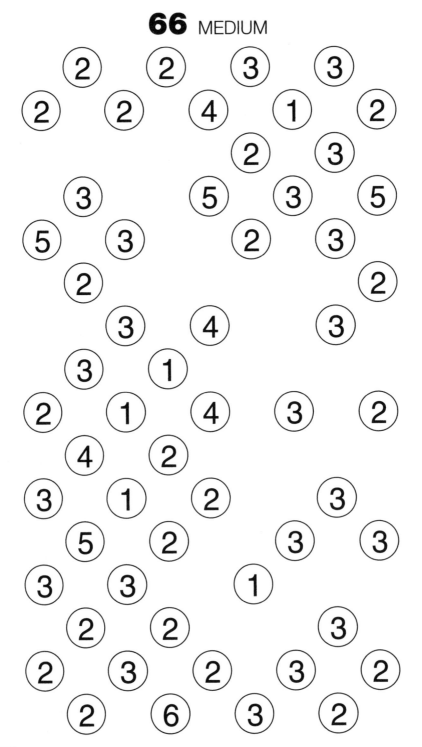

67 MEDIUM

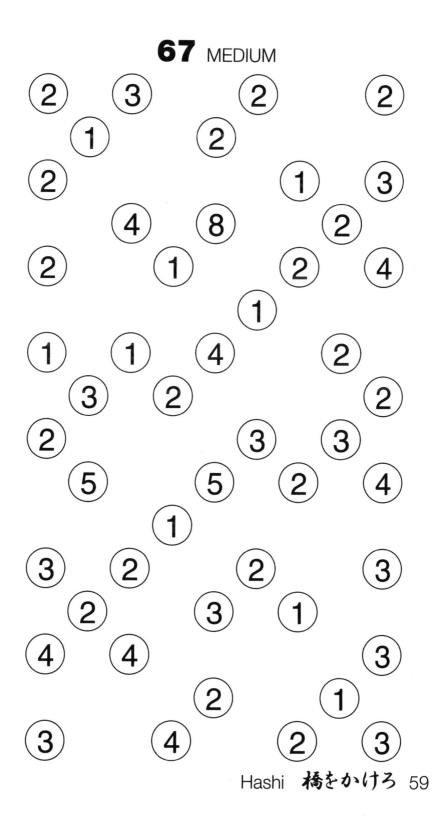

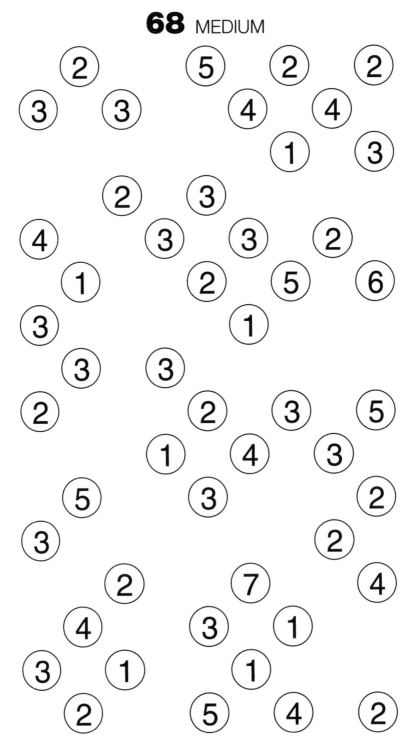

69 MEDIUM

1 2 2 3 2 2
1 2
3 3 3 3 1
3 1 2
3 4 1
3 2 4
5 2 3
2 3
3 4 1 1 1 1 5
3 4
3 3 1 3
2 2 4 1
5 2
2 1 3 3 3 5 4
4 2
3 3 4
4 3 2
3 3 3 2
4 2
1 1 2 3 4
1 1
2 2 3 3 2 3

③ ⑤ ② ④ ①
① ③ ② ① ②
② ③ ① ④ ②
① ② ②
② ③ ②
② ① ③ ②
② ②
② ② ④ ③ ② ④
① ③ ③
② ② ②
② ② ③ ④ ⑤
② ① ② ① ③
③ ③ ③
③ ② ①
① ③ ⑤ ③ ② ②
② ⑤
① ③ ② ①
① ③ ②
③ ③ ①
③ ② ① ① ④
① ① ② ④ ②
③ ② ② ② ③

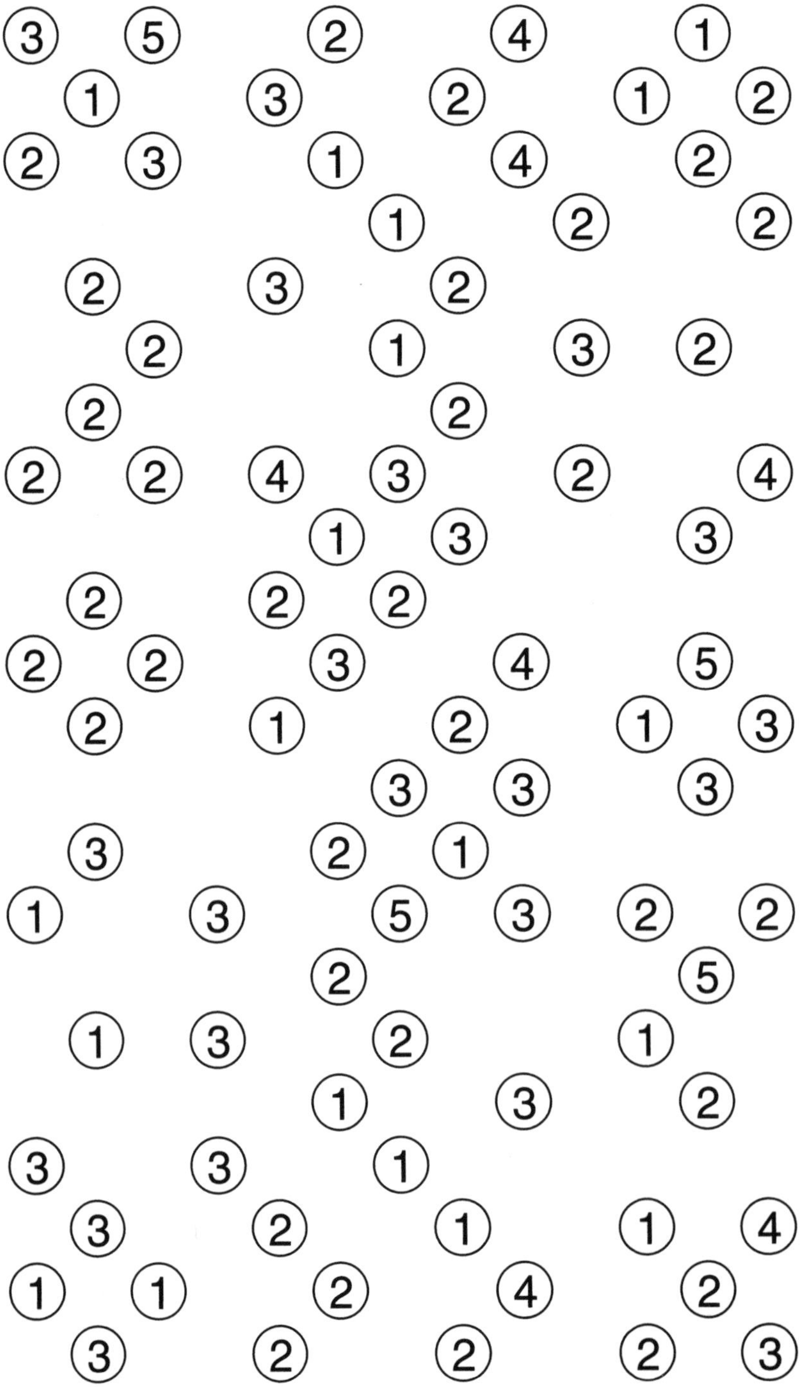

② ③ ② ② ① ①

③ ③ ⑥ ①

① ② ③

② ② ② ③ ②

① ②

① ④ ④ ③

③ ① ① ③ ④

② ②

③ ② ② ③

② ③ ③ ④

⑤ ④ ① ③ ③ ②

③ ③

① ② ①

③ ③ ② ③ ⑦ ③

②

③ ③ ③ ① ③

③ ⑤ ③ ②

③ ④ ③

③ ③ ① ① ④

① ② ② ①

② ④ ② ③ ③ ②

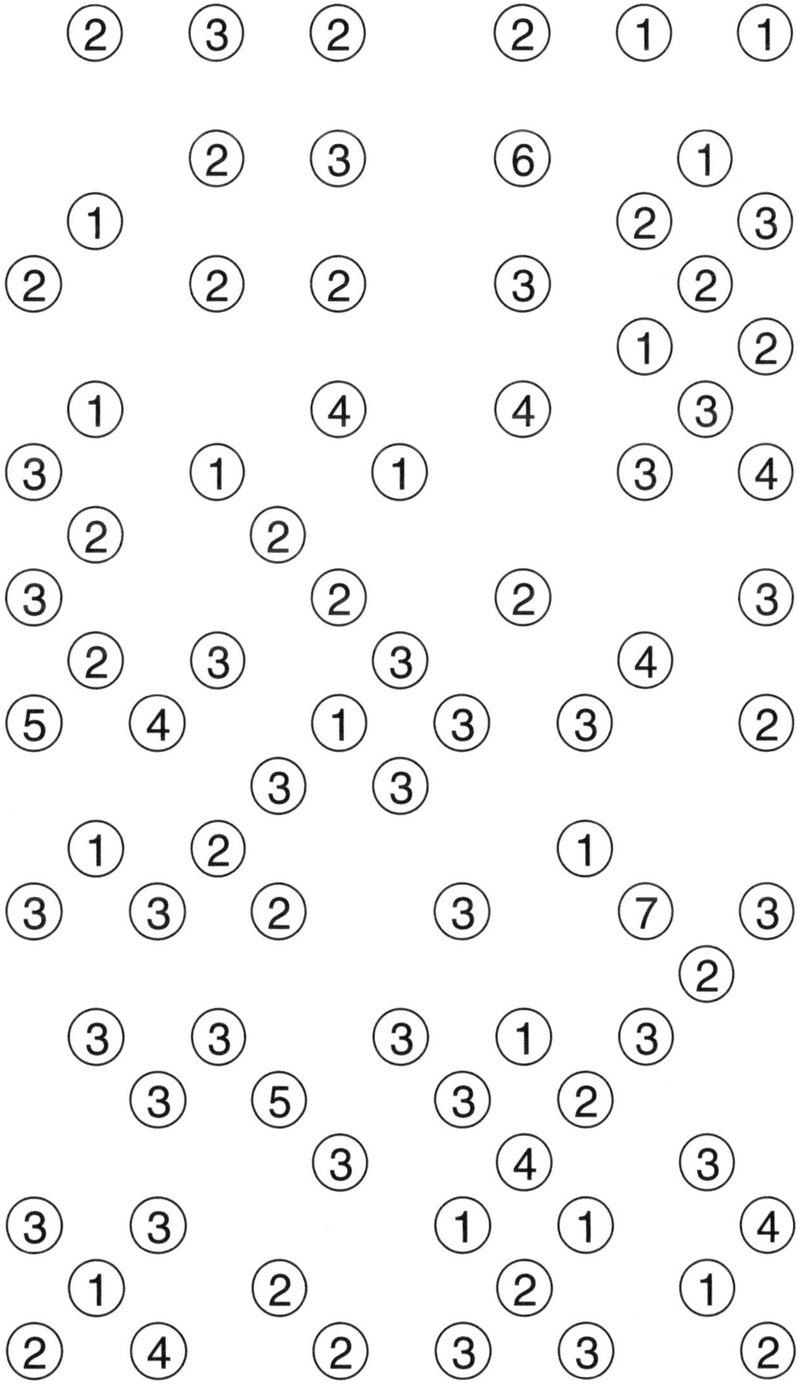

72 HARD

	1		3		2		1		4			2
3		1		1		3		1		2		
	3		3		2		1		3			
3		3		2		3				4		3
	1		2		4			4			2	
4		3		2		1				1		3
									3		2	
5			3			3		4				
	1			4			1		3			4
2		2				3		2			1	
	2				2		3		2			3
1		2		2		4		4			3	
	3		2		2		2			2		3
3				3		3					1	
	1		3					4		2		
3		3		2			2		3		4	
	1		4		3			2		1		
1		2							2		1	
	3		5			5		3		3		3
3		1			1		1					
						2		3			2	
2			3		2		3			3		2

73 HARD

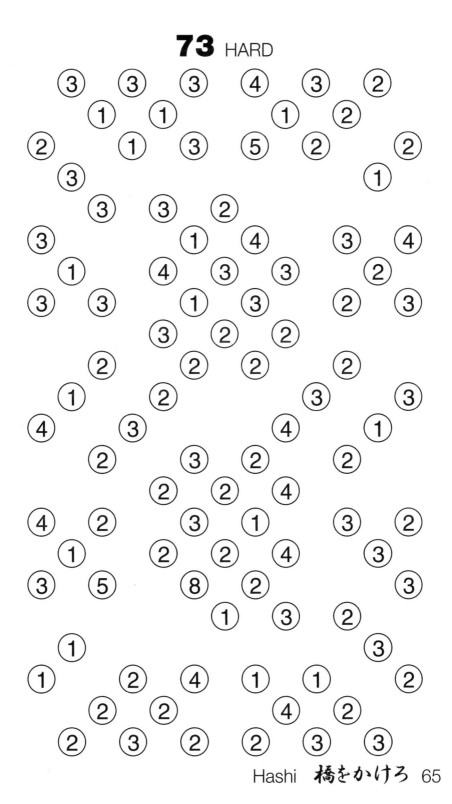

74 HARD

3		2			2		3			3		2
	1		4			3		3			1	
3		1							2			2
					3			2			3	
	2		4			2			3			3
4		4			3		2			2		
	1			3		3		3			4	
1		3			2		3			3		4
	2										1	
2		3		4		2		3		4		2
	3		1		1							
							3		3		2	
3		3		8		5		2		4		4
	3										2	
2		1			3		4			3		3
	3			3		1		2			5	
		1			3		3			1		2
3			2			3			4		2	
	2			4			3					
3			1							1		3
	2			4		1			3		1	
3		3			2		4			3		3

75 HARD

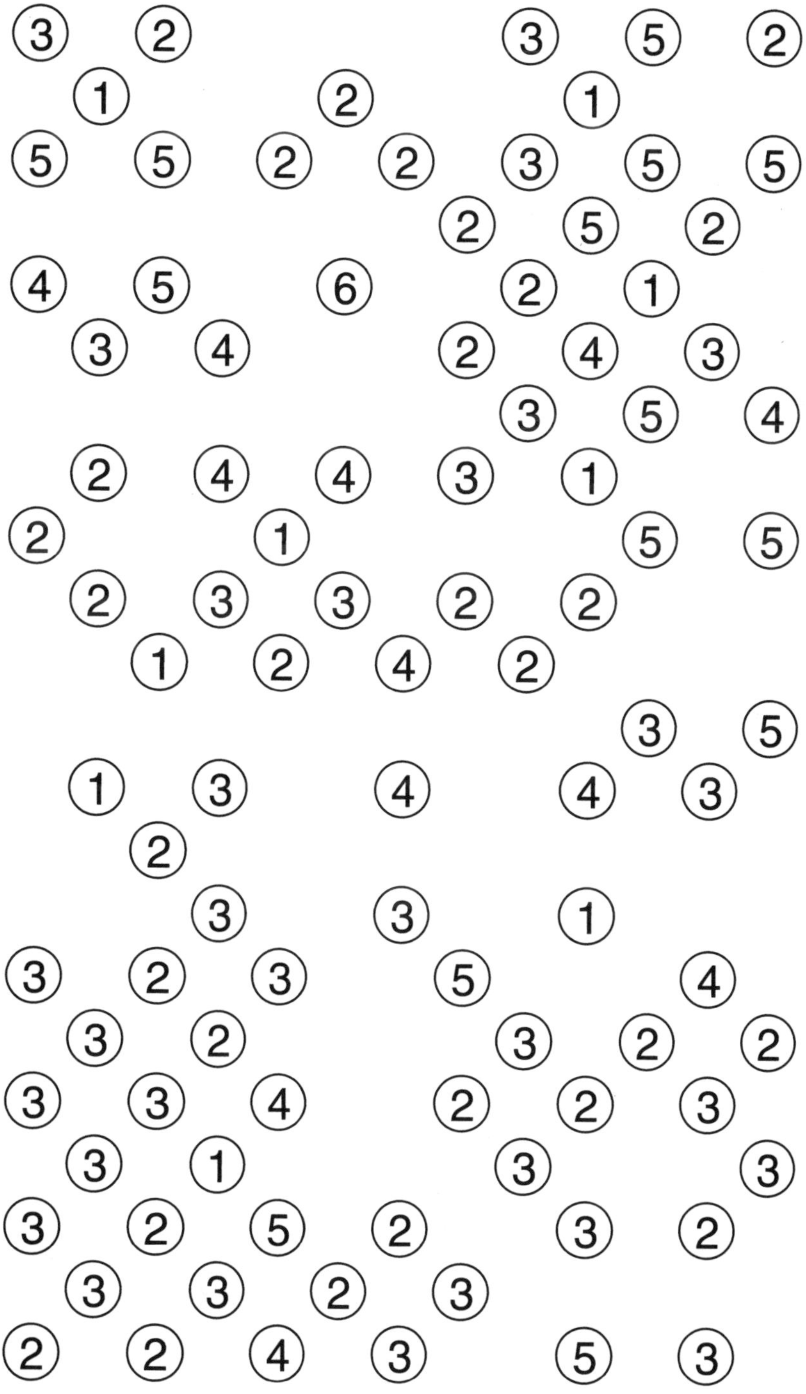

③ ③ ③ ③ ② ② ①
      ①   ②   ②
② ③ ② ② ③ ③
    ②   ③ ③ ③ ⑤ ② ①
   ③   ③
②   ① ② ③ ③ ②
    ③   ③ ① ③
③ ③   ②
    ③   ⑤ ③ ② ③
⑤ ② ③ ③ ①   ①
       ② ③ ⑤ ⑤
③ ⑤ ① ② ①
   ②   ①   ②
  ① ⑦ ③ ③ ①
② ① ③ ④ ③ ① ③
        ③ ⑦ ③ ⑤
④ ④ ⑤ ③
  ③ ① ② ③ ④ ① ③
  ③ ③ ② ③ ①
③   ② ①
   ② ④ ① ② ③
  ④ ② ① ②
   ② ② ③ ③ ③ ④
② ① ④ ③ ①
  ②   ① ④
   ③ ⑤ ④ ⑤
  ① ③ ③ ② ② ⑤
③   ①
  ③ ③ ② ① ② ⑤ ②
  ① ⑤ ② ① ② ④
③ ① ②
  ② ③ ⑤ ③ ④ ④ ②

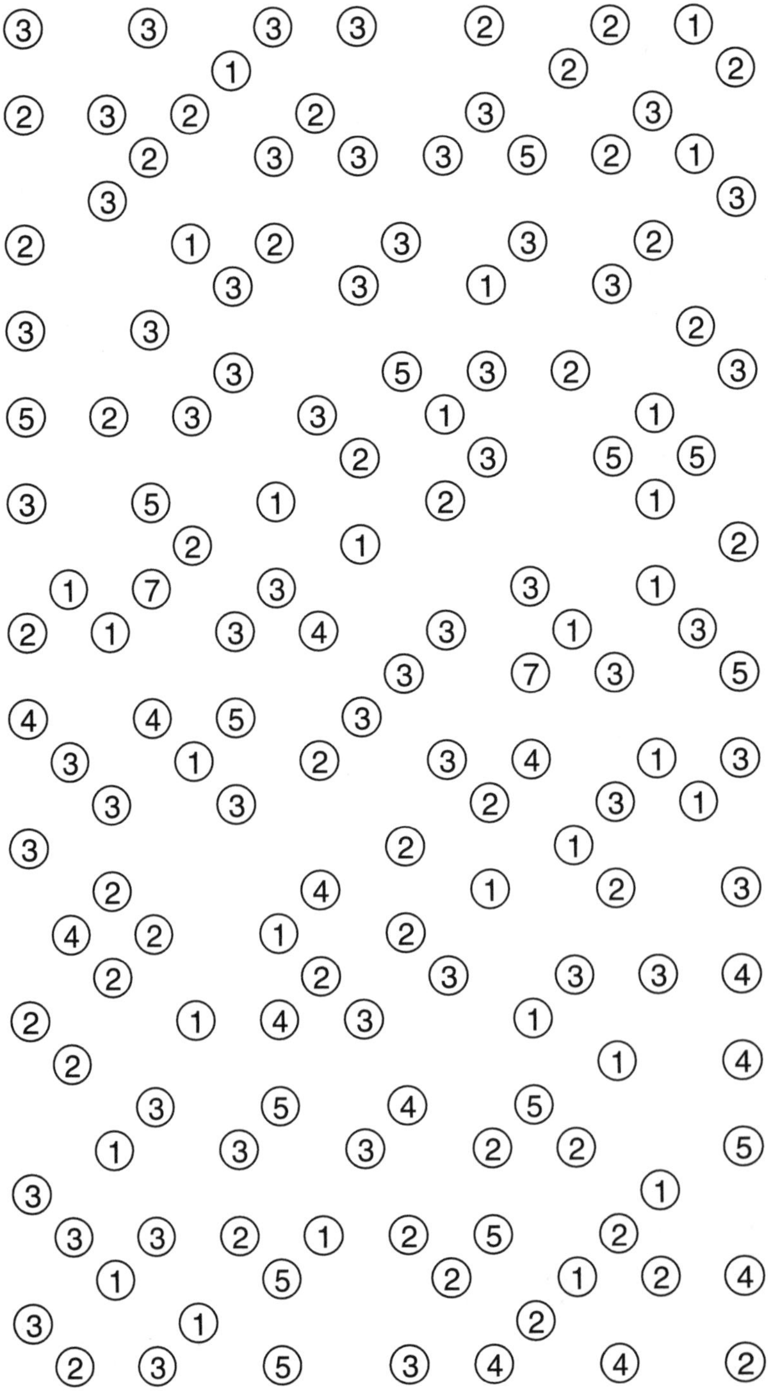

77 HARD

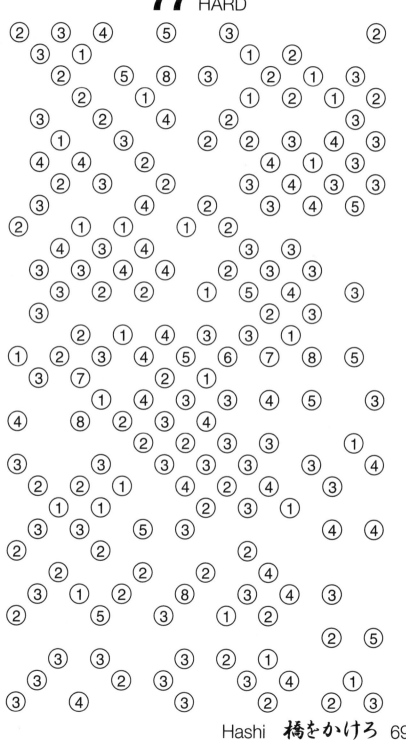

78 HARD

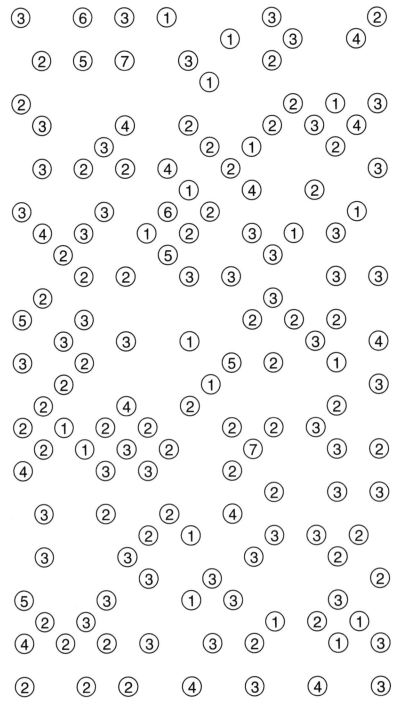

HEYAWAKE

In a heyawake puzzle, the grid is divided by dark lines into many different "rooms." Some rooms contain a number, which indicates the number of black cells inside that room. (Rooms without a number may include any number of black squares, including zero.) Black squares may not lie horizontally or vertically adjacent to another black square. The white squares must all remain connected to each other, and no unbroken line of white cells may extend into more than two rooms; the line must be blocked by a black cell when it reaches a third room.

The diagram at right, which represents the corner of a larger grid, shows some examples of illegal cell placements. The two areas marked with X's in the lower left both break the rules—they're sections of white cells that are cut off from the white cells in the rest of the grid. In the upper right, two black cells are adjacent, which is also illegal.

Let's try solving a heyawake puzzle together so you can get the hang of it. Experienced heyawake solvers would be able to shade in a number of squares right away, giving you a grid that looks like the one seen below right. (Dots represent squares that can't possibly be shaded black.) How would they know to fill in the grid this way?

Start by taking a look at the room in the upper left of the grid, with a 2 in it. There are three adjacent cells in that room, and from the number 2, we know that two of them must be shaded black. No two black squares can be adjacent, so the center square must be white, and the other two squares shaded black. A dot can be placed in the center square to indicate that it's definitely white, as well as in the squares adjacent to the black squares just colored in. A dot can also be placed in the second square of the second row, since if that square were colored black, it would cut off the white square above it from the rest of the grid, which is illegal.

Now let's move to the upper right, where we see a 2×2 room with a 2 in it. There are two ways to place two black squares in this room: along the upper-left-to-lower-right diagonal, or along the lower-left-to-upper-right diagonal. However, the first of those arrangements creates a white square in the corner that's cut off from the rest of the grid, so the other arrangement is the correct one. After shading in the black squares, we can surround the black squares with dots, and also place dots in the two squares that would create isolated white squares if they were shaded in.

One more room, and then we'll be caught up. Look at the 2×3 room with a 3 in it, along the bottom edge of the grid. To shade in three squares without placing two black squares next to each other, the black squares will need to be placed in a V shape, facing one of two directions. If the V points away from the wall, that creates a single white square that's cut off from the rest of the grid. Therefore the V points toward the wall, and we can once again surround the black squares with dots. We can also place dots in the fifth and seventh squares of the fifth row, since shading either square would divide the grid into two separate sections.

Now there are no rooms with numbers remaining. What can we do next? Remember that a line of white squares cannot extend through more than two rooms. There are three squares in the grid that we can shade in thanks to this rule. In the second row, the fourth square must be shaded in, preventing the three white cells to the left from extending into a third room. Similarly, black squares can be placed in the last square of the fourth row, and the third square of the fifth row. After surrounding those black squares with dots, the grid looks like this.

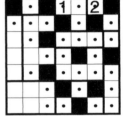

Adding those dots has not created any rows of white squares long enough to allow us to place more black squares, so what now? Well, take a look at the fifth square in the third row. That square can't be black, or it would divide the grid into two isolated areas. Once we place a dot in it, now we have two squares we can fill in to block rows of white squares from extending into a third room. Here's what the puzzle looks like after that.

Can you see what to do next? Much like the last step, there's one square we can place a dot in, because shading it in would divide the grid into two separate sections. It's the second square of the fourth row. Adding a dot there once again creates two lines of white squares that extend through two rooms, so we can cap those lines with black squares. Every remaining square must be white, since each one is either adjacent to a newly shaded-in black square, or would divide the grid into two isolated areas. And we're done!

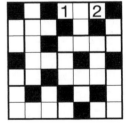

79 EASY

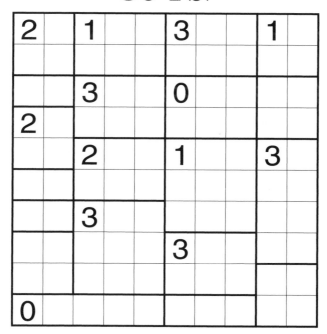

80 EASY

81 EASY

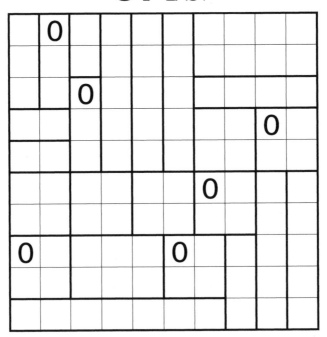

82 EASY

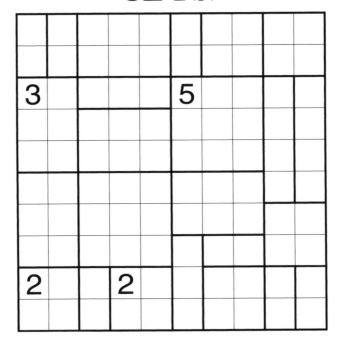

83 EASY

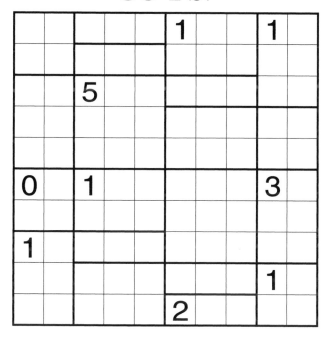

84 EASY

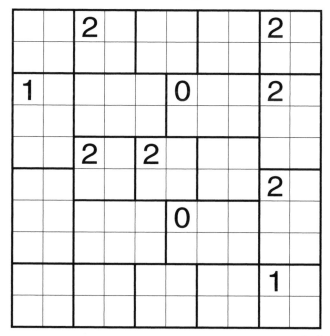

85 EASY

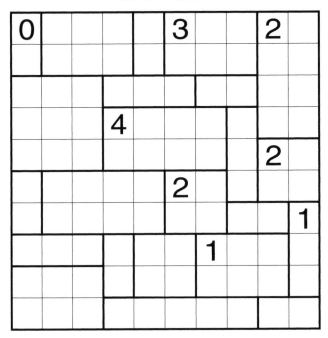

86 EASY

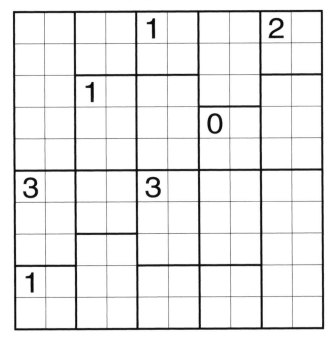

87 EASY

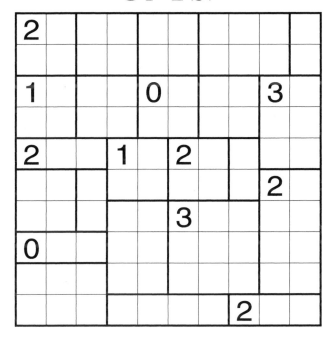

88 EASY

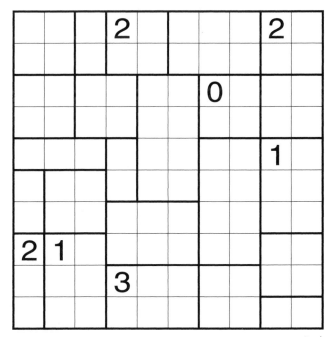

89 EASY

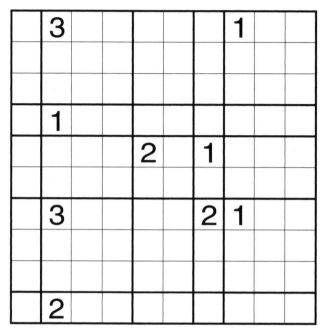

90 EASY

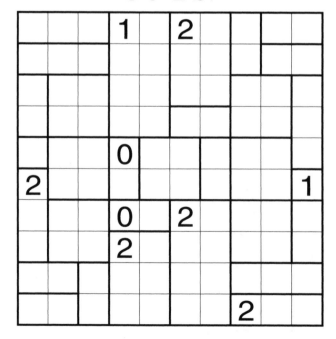

91 MEDIUM

92 MEDIUM

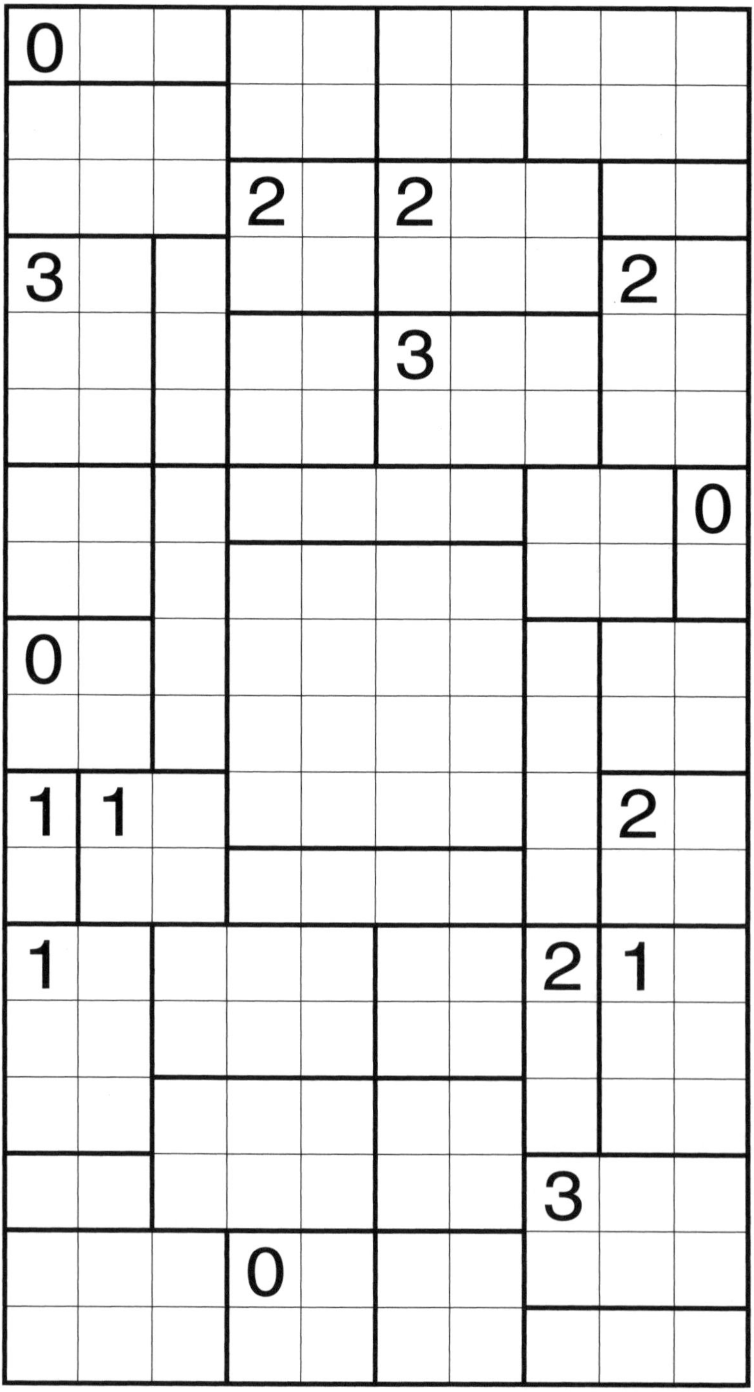

MEDIUM

		0		1			
						2	
		1		3			
2	2			3			3
	3			2			
		2		3			
2				2		0	
1		2		2			

95 MEDIUM

96 MEDIUM

97 MEDIUM

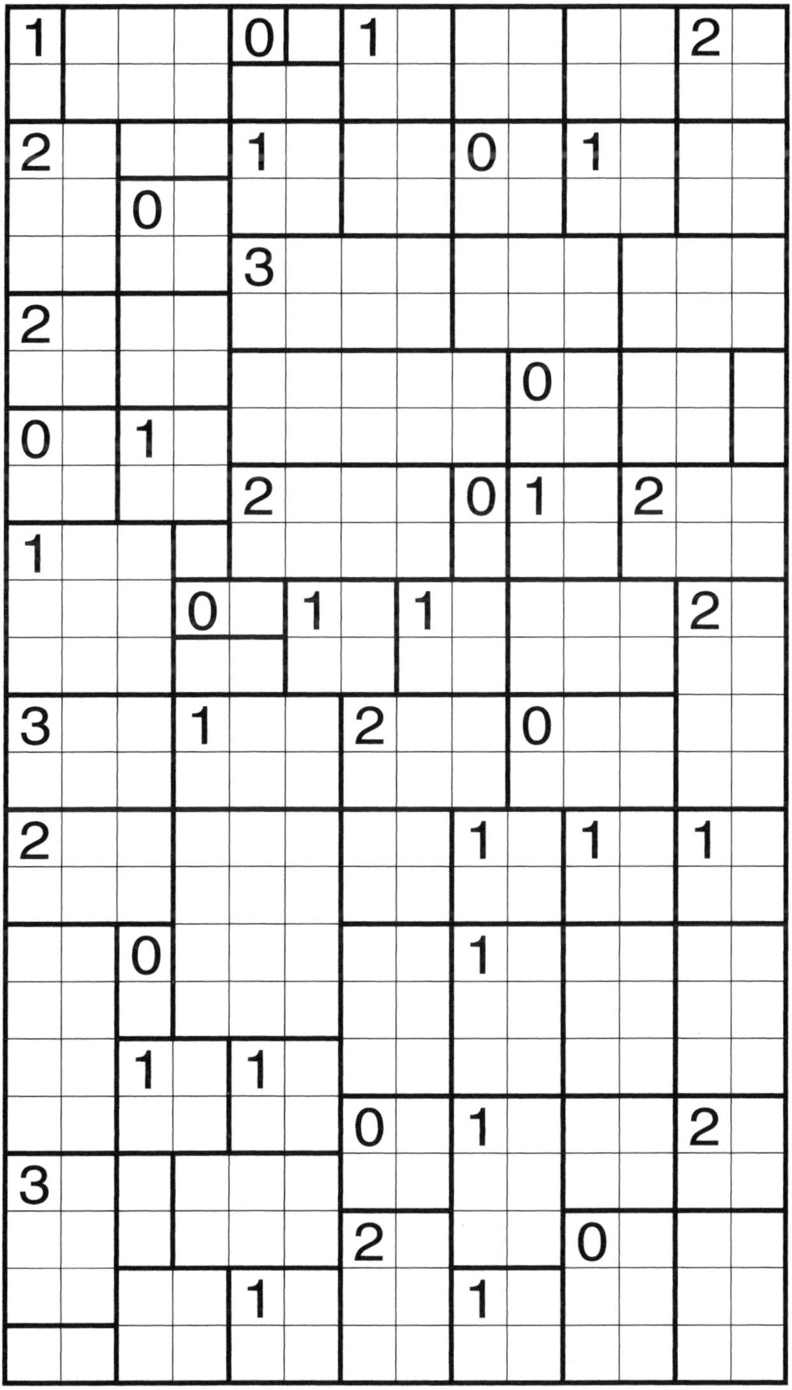

1	2	2		2		2		
2				1	0			0
	2						1	
		2		2				
2	3				1	1		0
1		3		1				
	1					3		
1		4		5				
2	2							
1		1						
	1							
					1		0	
	3	2		1		2		
2		2	2	1				
	1					1		
			1					

99 HARD

100 HARD

1	1		3	0			1
				2	2		1
3	2		1		4		1
	1		0				
1	1		2		0		2
	2						0
	4		2	3	2		1
	2		2		1		2
	1				1		

101 HARD

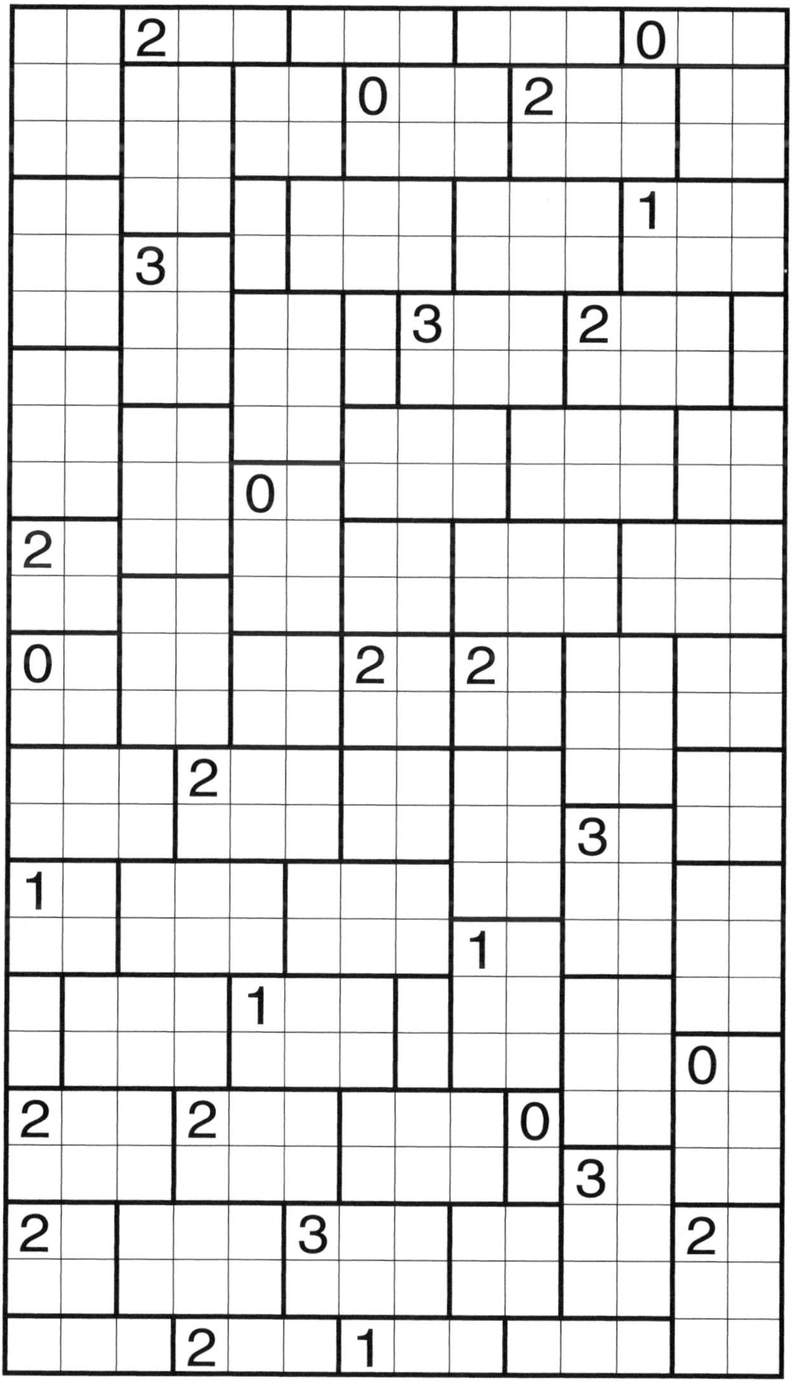

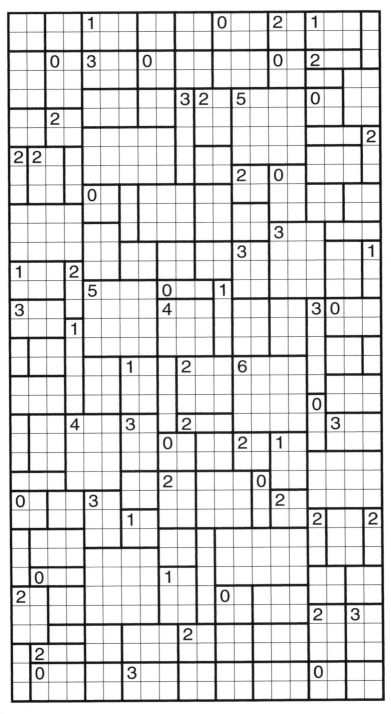

103 HARD

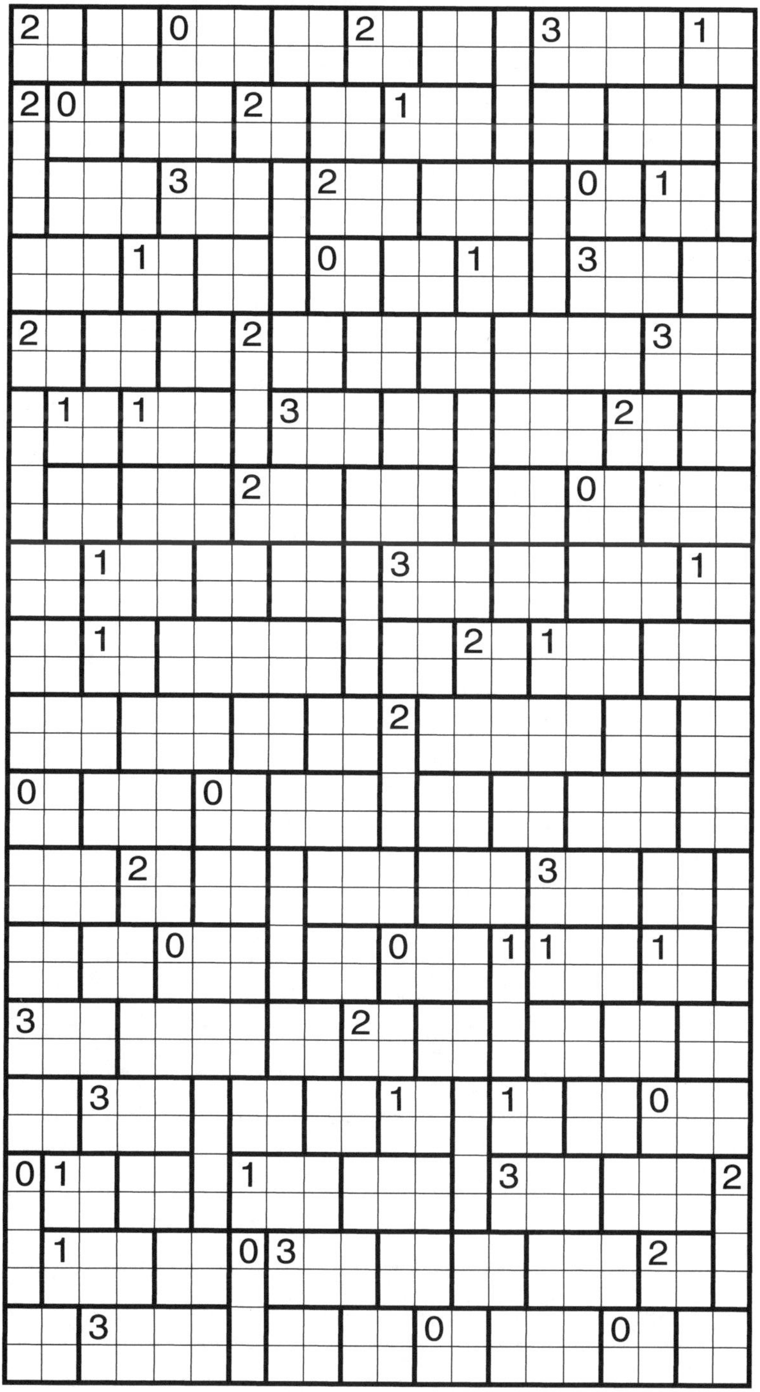

104 HARD

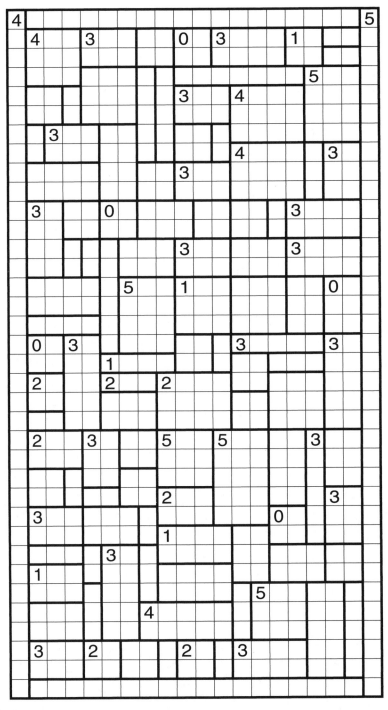

HITORI

In a hitori puzzle, the grid is filled with numbers, many of which appear multiple times in various rows and columns. Your task as the solver is to remove numbers by shading them in, so that each number appears only once in any row or column, no two shaded squares are horizontally or vertically adjacent, and all the unshaded squares remain connected to each other. (That is, a path may be traced between any two unshaded squares, passing only through other horizontally and vertically adjacent unshaded squares; squeezing diagonally between two shaded squares isn't legal.)

Here's a small hitori puzzle as an example. There are a few easy deductions we can make to start with. See those three adjacent 3s in the second row? When you see three identical adjacent numbers like that, you can always shade in the two on the outside (circling the one on the inside to indicate that you've identified it as an unshaded square). Why? Well, we know that each row and column can't have the same number appear in it more than once. If the leftmost or rightmost 3 were unshaded, the other two would have to be shaded—which would mean two shaded squares were directly adjacent to each other, which is against the rules. Therefore, the middle 3 must be unshaded. This is a common pattern, and a good one to look out for when starting a puzzle.

Now that we've shaded in two squares, we know that any square adjacent to the shaded-in squares must be unshaded, and we can circle those numbers to indicate that. After doing that, we should check the rows and columns those numbers are in to see if, given our new information, we can locate any new squares to shade in. Most of the numbers are already the only instance of those digits in their rows and columns, but the two 1s in the upper left each share a row or column with the 1 in the upper left corner, so we can shade that square in.

Now, using the rule that all unshaded squares must stay connected, we can locate two more unshaded squares. If the 3 in the leftmost column were shaded in, there would then be three black squares surrounding the unshaded 1 above it, blocking it off from the rest of the grid. So that 3 must be unshaded. Similarly, the 4 in the top row must also be unshaded (which means that the 4 below it in the same column can be shaded in, and the numbers around it circled).

None of those circled numbers automatically lead to more shaded-in squares, so we'll need to look elsewhere to make deductions. Notice the 2×2 square of 2s in the lower left corner of the grid. Is the square in the corner shaded or unshaded? If it's unshaded, then the square above it and the square to its right must be shaded, which would isolate that square from the rest of the board. That can't be the case, so it must be shaded, which means the two adjacent squares are unshaded, and the fourth 2 in that corner is shaded, giving us a grid that looks like this.

What next? There's another 2×2 square of 6s along the bottom of the grid. That square will have to contain two black squares, going either diagonally from the top left to the bottom right, or the bottom left to the top right. If it's the first of those two options, that would divide the grid into two sections and block off a triangle of squares in the lower left. (Another way to think of this rule is to look for diagonally connected lines of black squares that touch one wall of the grid. Any chain like that can never touch another wall of the grid. Shading in the upper left and lower right 6s would extend the existing chain of black squares back to the wall.) This can't be the case, so the lower left and upper right 6s must be shaded and the other 6s circled (as well as the 3s next to the upper right black square). We can also circle the two 5s adjacent to the 2s in the lower left corner, as we did with the 3 and 4 in the upper left. The circled 5 in the leftmost column is adjacent to another 5, so we can shade that in, and now we're getting close.

You may already have spotted the 4 on the bottom of the grid that can't be shaded in; circle it, and shade in the 4 in the same column (and circle the numbers in the adjacent squares, of course—the 2 above it and the 2 to its right). Now there's a chain of three black squares connected to the bottom of the grid, and getting close to the right edge. It can't touch the right edge, so circle the two squares that would cause it to connect to the edge. One of those squares lets you shade in two more squares—there are other 7s in the same row and column as the 7 you just circled. Shade those in and circle any squares next to them that aren't already circled.

Almost there. The chains of black squares extending from the upper left and lower left corners of the grid are coming dangerously close to meeting at the 6 in the third square of third row. Circle that 6 and shade in the 6 at the end of the row. After you circle the two 5s next to that 6, you'll see that they're next to another 5, which you can shade in. Every remaining square is either next to a black square or would divide the grid into two sections if it were shaded in, so all the remaining numbers must be unshaded. And we're done!

As you solve more hitori, you'll find new solving techniques besides these. Keep an eye out for repeated numbers (since they may indicate a part of the grid where you can make a deduction), and remember to check when you circle a number to see if there are any repeats of that number in the same row or column that you can shade in. Have fun!

105 EASY

4	3	4	2	4	4	7	3
5	1	8	4	2	3	6	4
5	6	5	4	7	2	8	7
4	2	2	4	3	1	1	7
3	2	2	6	8	1	1	5
7	5	3	6	1	7	2	6
3	7	3	5	3	6	6	3
1	4	6	7	5	8	3	2

106 EASY

8	2	5	1	1	1	3	6
2	4	8	2	3	5	1	7
6	3	7	1	7	8	2	3
5	3	6	8	2	2	7	6
2	3	4	5	3	3	4	1
7	8	2	4	5	6	1	4
3	5	1	6	5	4	8	8
4	8	6	3	7	1	8	8

107 EASY

5	3	1	1	1	8	2	5
6	3	5	2	7	6	1	4
8	1	5	7	8	2	3	4
1	3	7	4	5	4	6	8
3	4	2	6	7	7	7	2
4	2	6	3	8	1	5	7
2	7	3	5	2	2	8	5
7	6	8	8	8	3	4	5

108 EASY

1	1	3	2	5	7	8	5
2	2	4	8	3	7	1	5
3	4	3	7	6	2	5	5
7	5	6	4	2	1	4	1
4	7	8	1	5	3	6	4
5	6	8	4	1	6	3	2
6	3	1	8	4	5	7	6
1	5	2	3	8	8	7	8

109 EASY

1	1	3	4	2	5	4	1
1	1	4	6	4	3	2	8
2	4	5	5	7	3	3	3
3	2	6	1	4	2	5	7
2	2	7	5	2	8	7	6
4	3	2	2	8	7	6	7
8	3	1	4	7	6	7	5
8	5	4	7	6	8	8	8

110 EASY

3	2	1	3	2	4	2	6
1	8	6	6	2	8	7	3
8	1	2	6	5	7	5	4
3	5	8	1	1	1	2	5
5	3	4	4	7	2	3	7
4	8	7	2	8	3	5	6
2	5	1	7	6	6	4	1
5	8	4	5	7	2	3	4

111 EASY

6	3	4	2	5	7	8	1
3	6	3	5	1	4	3	2
7	3	5	8	1	8	6	4
2	2	2	6	1	3	4	5
4	5	7	1	3	2	2	2
5	8	3	1	2	6	4	7
2	5	8	1	4	7	1	3
8	7	6	3	6	1	5	4

112 EASY

1	3	4	4	4	5	8	5
5	6	1	7	8	2	4	2
3	7	8	6	7	4	2	3
8	6	5	5	2	8	1	3
1	2	3	8	6	7	7	4
8	1	2	2	3	6	6	7
3	4	2	2	5	1	5	8
3	8	6	7	4	2	3	1

113 EASY

6	2	5	8	5	4	3	1
1	6	3	3	2	5	1	4
4	2	8	5	3	1	6	7
5	3	4	1	7	7	7	2
7	4	4	4	6	3	2	1
8	1	6	7	5	2	6	3
8	2	7	5	4	1	5	3
8	4	7	2	7	6	1	5

114 EASY

6	8	8	7	2	3	8	1
2	4	3	2	6	1	7	5
4	3	2	8	8	7	3	4
4	6	1	5	2	6	3	8
4	1	4	2	3	8	2	7
3	5	4	1	2	4	6	5
5	5	2	4	7	6	8	3
6	7	5	5	4	1	1	8

115 EASY

1	1	2	3	4	6	7	8
1	1	7	3	4	8	6	5
2	4	2	8	3	1	5	6
3	5	6	8	7	7	2	6
5	2	5	6	5	4	8	1
7	1	1	8	2	3	6	8
4	7	3	1	5	2	6	8
2	8	5	7	1	6	3	2

116 EASY

5	6	5	8	4	7	4	1
7	1	1	1	2	2	3	3
6	5	7	2	8	3	1	4
3	2	8	1	6	4	6	7
1	7	4	7	3	5	8	2
6	4	8	5	8	1	2	3
8	3	6	3	1	5	7	2
4	8	7	6	4	2	1	5

5	11	5	3	1	2	10	9	8	6	10	7
3	1	1	1	4	7	11	6	10	7	12	8
5	7	5	4	10	11	2	1	9	8	2	6
9	9	2	12	3	12	6	7	1	2	8	7
9	9	6	8	3	1	4	10	7	5	7	3
4	6	3	4	7	4	1	4	2	4	5	4
1	8	8	5	10	12	6	2	7	3	9	11
2	8	8	9	5	5	12	11	3	1	6	10
11	12	4	2	5	5	7	11	5	9	4	1
10	4	7	6	12	3	9	4	5	8	1	2
7	3	12	1	2	10	3	5	12	11	9	8
6	1	10	6	12	4	5	7	8	2	11	9

1	10	8	4	2	5	8	7	9	6	3	4
1	2	6	5	7	10	3	4	2	7	3	9
4	12	12	12	7	6	9	2	10	3	8	2
9	6	10	2	8	9	8	1	10	4	5	5
9	7	5	3	8	10	10	2	1	6	4	6
8	4	2	1	10	7	2	10	4	5	2	3
2	10	9	7	5	3	1	6	8	9	7	10
2	3	5	10	9	4	8	8	6	2	1	10
5	9	4	3	1	2	7	8	3	8	4	6
5	5	3	7	10	8	1	9	5	10	2	1
6	8	4	4	10	5	2	3	5	1	9	4
3	6	7	9	8	1	5	4	2	3	6	8

11	2	2	5	5	9	9	7	10	6	3	3
5	2	3	11	11	12	9	9	7	4	12	1
10	5	12	11	1	8	3	9	9	2	11	6
2	3	4	8	10	12	5	1	9	9	6	7
12	12	8	2	2	5	1	4	11	9	7	7
9	12	8	2	2	1	3	10	2	7	5	11
7	10	5	9	12	6	6	8	1	11	4	4
11	1	2	7	6	6	2	8	8	10	4	4
1	4	7	6	6	2	4	5	8	8	10	12
10	9	6	6	7	7	12	12	3	8	8	5
4	6	6	10	9	7	7	2	5	11	8	8
3	6	10	10	3	11	1	4	2	12	9	8

1	8	6	3	3	3	11	2	12	7	5	9
10	11	5	7	1	6	9	3	3	2	4	12
6	1	6	3	7	2	12	6	4	6	10	5
5	12	4	4	8	1	5	6	2	9	8	3
3	3	1	4	9	8	2	8	11	5	7	10
12	3	7	5	7	2	6	7	1	2	9	11
4	7	2	11	6	7	1	5	3	8	11	11
11	9	10	6	11	3	4	2	10	10	1	5
2	6	12	8	5	11	2	1	9	12	4	8
6	8	5	9	12	6	10	4	7	3	1	9
7	1	11	8	2	9	12	10	5	4	3	1
4	10	3	7	2	4	8	5	7	6	12	4

5	8	4	4	12	7	3	3	3	2	10	11
1	1	4	4	3	6	10	9	5	6	7	12
1	1	3	7	6	6	12	10	2	11	5	5
11	2	1	3	10	4	7	6	7	9	5	5
7	9	9	9	5	12	8	1	1	1	4	2
2	4	2	1	2	9	7	12	7	5	11	3
4	10	10	10	9	12	6	8	8	8	3	11
12	3	5	8	1	10	7	2	7	4	6	11
3	6	6	6	8	5	5	5	11	12	2	9
8	12	8	11	4	5	4	7	6	10	2	10
10	7	7	12	11	5	1	4	7	3	2	6
6	7	7	2	4	8	4	11	9	10	1	10

122 MEDIUM

3	2	12	8	10	2	6	5	7	8	4	4
1	1	1	2	1	4	10	9	9	11	7	6
8	2	10	5	4	5	12	9	9	6	1	5
9	4	9	6	3	7	3	2	12	10	10	8
7	7	11	1	12	9	1	5	6	10	10	3
7	7	5	1	8	2	6	4	9	3	9	6
4	8	3	12	6	6	5	3	10	9	11	2
2	6	3	12	7	1	11	8	2	4	4	9
6	5	2	3	5	10	8	11	4	9	12	5
6	3	7	11	8	1	4	7	2	5	2	10
10	5	6	7	2	8	4	1	8	1	3	11
1	11	7	10	1	12	7	6	5	8	5	4

11	2	4	5	12	2	2	1	5	6	3	7
10	1	9	7	9	8	6	11	3	10	6	11
8	4	1	10	3	5	9	11	6	4	10	12
7	9	8	10	7	6	12	7	11	12	2	3
4	11	7	5	2	1	12	10	2	11	1	8
1	2	3	4	5	6	7	8	9	10	11	12
12	11	10	9	8	7	6	5	4	3	2	1
3	8	6	4	8	2	1	11	5	9	12	4
8	12	10	2	3	4	8	6	12	7	5	5
7	5	11	9	10	9	3	1	4	1	8	7
2	9	12	1	11	10	2	4	8	12	7	6
6	6	2	7	7	10	4	8	1	5	4	10

8	6	3	4	3	12	8	9	2	11	5	5
12	11	8	2	6	10	9	4	3	7	5	5
7	4	6	8	10	11	2	10	5	3	6	9
9	5	12	7	11	2	3	7	4	2	8	8
4	12	3	11	9	3	1	8	5	6	7	2
5	11	9	2	7	2	6	2	8	12	4	12
10	7	3	9	8	6	12	11	5	4	2	3
6	5	10	2	12	5	11	4	7	2	3	9
10	9	4	12	4	5	4	3	10	8	9	6
3	8	6	11	5	9	7	8	12	9	10	11
4	2	11	10	3	8	1	12	6	5	11	7
11	7	7	7	8	10	5	6	6	2	12	2

125 HARD

8	11	1	7	9	12	11	5	6	2	10	10
10	9	1	6	8	7	3	7	2	4	12	12
1	1	1	11	10	2	8	9	4	8	7	6
5	9	6	1	4	3	12	3	10	9	1	2
8	12	11	3	8	9	10	2	1	10	4	11
2	4	10	6	1	4	6	4	8	5	9	3
7	10	4	2	5	11	5	12	3	8	6	9
11	3	5	12	6	8	1	8	4	3	12	7
7	8	2	10	9	5	2	6	1	12	3	6
3	6	8	1	12	1	4	11	6	7	9	5
1	3	4	8	10	6	7	1	9	2	11	4
12	3	9	5	2	1	11	10	5	6	5	8

3	6	9	11	1	2	12	7	2	8	2	3
1	5	3	9	4	8	12	10	11	5	7	12
3	9	10	8	2	4	3	4	12	6	5	6
5	7	8	3	3	6	9	2	7	4	1	11
8	10	5	12	3	6	8	7	1	11	3	2
2	4	7	12	9	9	10	5	4	3	8	1
9	1	1	7	5	11	1	3	8	2	10	7
12	8	2	10	8	3	5	12	6	11	1	9
9	11	4	1	10	7	7	8	10	2	6	3
6	12	6	5	4	1	11	5	3	9	8	10
3	3	10	4	6	5	1	11	5	1	4	2
6	3	6	11	8	10	2	9	9	7	9	4

9	1	1	5	10	7	6	3	1	2	4	8
3	11	4	2	10	7	2	1	5	11	8	5
4	8	3	7	2	5	9	11	4	10	6	1
6	3	8	4	9	2	1	1	3	5	10	11
8	5	3	10	6	4	8	2	9	1	7	7
11	9	10	3	6	8	5	4	7	4	1	2
10	9	9	11	6	1	4	8	2	6	3	5
1	4	6	2	7	3	11	10	10	10	5	8
11	6	1	8	11	10	4	5	2	7	3	9
5	10	11	1	4	9	7	9	6	3	2	10
2	3	2	4	1	9	10	7	11	5	6	8
1	2	7	6	3	8	3	6	8	5	9	4

12	5	6	6	15	1	3	13	16	11	11	12	14	8	9	7	4
16	17	6	6	5	8	7	10	14	11	11	9	9	15	3	3	13
13	13	1	15	4	14	6	4	6	3	16	10	10	7	8	9	9
13	13	17	7	8	7	12	2	5	10	14	16	6	5	15	9	9
11	4	14	9	3	17	3	12	9	2	15	7	13	6	16	8	5
3	1	12	10	2	6	14	9	8	8	9	15	7	17	16	1	4
2	2	11	11	17	9	9	3	7	14	10	8	13	12	16	15	6
5	15	2	12	10	11	17	1	1	1	4	11	16	6	13	7	3
15	7	5	8	12	10	16	1	1	17	8	5	3	13	2	14	4
14	9	13	13	12	4	10	1	17	4	2	15	3	9	7	6	16
11	12	14	4	17	15	16	9	7	5	10	13	3	2	1	6	8
4	10	10	16	13	13	11	5	12	6	6	7	15	14	14	2	2
1	10	10	14	13	13	8	6	11	16	15	4	11	3	17	2	2
8	8	16	1	1	3	15	10	2	12	13	3	17	11	5	5	14
6	3	9	5	7	16	14	11	2	15	3	14	17	4	12	10	10
9	16	3	3	7	5	2	15	13	13	17	1	12	1	11	10	10
9	11	3	3	6	5	5	16	13	7	12	17	14	10	2	4	15

L I T S

LITS puzzles involve placing shapes on a grid according to a simple set of rules. The four shapes are known by the letters "L," "I," "T," and "S" (named after the letter shapes they resemble); each of the four shapes is a tetromino, a polygon created by joining four squares together, just like a domino is a shape made up of two squares.

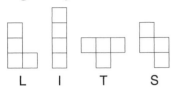

L   I   T   S

Each LITS puzzle contains a number of differently sized and shaped areas bounded by bold lines. The goal is to place one tetromino in each area (by shading the four squares taken up by each tetromino) such that three conditions are fulfilled. First, no tetromino may ever touch an identically shaped tetromino. So an L tetromino may touch an I, T, or S tetromino, but not another L tetromino. (Note that two L tetrominos could touch at a corner only, since touching diagonally does not count as being adjacent in a LITS puzzle.) Second, no 2×2 area of the grid may be completely shaded in. This is true whether or not the 2×2 area crosses bold lines or not: In any 2×2 square area of the grid, at least one square must remain unshaded. Finally, all the tetrominoes must be orthogonally connected to each other. (Another way to look at it is that once the puzzle is correctly completed, you must be able to travel from any shaded square to any other shaded square by moving horizontally or vertically from one shaded square to another, without ever being forced to pass through an unshaded square.)

That probably sounds more complicated than it actually is. Let's take a look at a small LITS puzzle and solve it together so you can see how it works.

The first thing we can do is look to see if there are any areas that contain exactly four squares. If there are, our job of shading four squares in each area is made easy: we can shade in all four squares in those areas right away. This grid has two such areas: one in the upper right that contains an S shape (in mirror image to the sample seen above), and one in the lower left that contains an L (rotated onto its side). Note that any of the four tetrominoes may appear in the

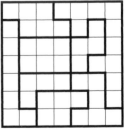

grid in any orientation, rotated or flipped over as necessary. The next step is to check to see if there are any 2×2 squares that are close to being completely filled in. And, in fact, there are—shading in the fifth square of the second row, the sixth square of the fourth row, or the third square of the sixth row would cause there to be a completely shaded 2×2 square. Therefore we know those squares must remain unshaded. We'll indicate that here by placing a dot in them, but you can indicate an unshaded square however you like.

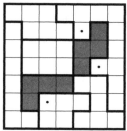

Now let's look at the five-square area on the bottom of the grid. We know the upper left square in it is unshaded, so the other four squares must be shaded. (That creates two more nearly filled 2×2 areas, so we can place dots indicating unshaded squares in the fifth squares of the fifth and bottom rows.) And what about that 2×3 rectangle near the center? What shape can it contain? Not an I; it's not tall or wide enough. Not an L or S, because there's no way to place an L that doesn't touch the L below it, and no way to place an S that doesn't touch the S to the right. (There's also no way to place an S that doesn't create a completely shaded 2×2 square.) That only leaves a T. It must be in the same orientation shown in the example, because if it were flipped 180 degrees, it would create two completely shaded 2×2 squares. Let's pause again and see what we've got.

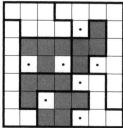

Okay! Turns out adding those two dots in the lower right has left exactly four squares in that area, so we can shade those in (and add a dot in the last square of the sixth row). And how about that long area on the left? There's only one way to place a shape that doesn't create a shaded 2×2 square; can you see where? It must be an I shape, placed as high as it can possibly go. If the highest shaded square in that area is lower than that, the shape must pass those two squares in the L tetromino, and it can't do that without making a 2×2 square. We can now draw a dot in the second square of the second row, and we're almost done: only two more shapes to place.

In the upper left, there are only five squares left, and we can eliminate the one in the lower right: if it's shaded in, so is the one to the left,

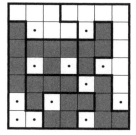

114

which makes a 2×2 square. So the other four squares contain an L tetromino. And what about the last area? If you check all the possibly ways to place a shape inside it, you'll see there's only one legal one: an I tetromino along the top edge of the grid. And we're done!

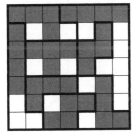

Now, you may have noticed we solved that puzzle without ever having to check if all the tetrominoes were connected. (They are, but we never had to use that rule to eliminate any possibilities.) That's okay—you may sometimes be able to solve a puzzle without using every single rule. But let's take a look at one other little puzzle so you can see that rule in action.

This might look impossible, with that huge open area at the top, but don't be daunted. We can fill in the lower left L shape right away. How about in the lower right? If the shape in it starts in the third square of the fourth row and proceeds around, it makes an L shape—but it touches the L shape to its left, so that's impossible. What if it starts in the square below it and continues to the right? That makes an L shape again, and it's still touching the other L shape, so that's no good, and that only leaves the arrangement shown here.

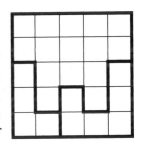

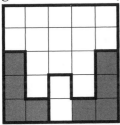

Now what? Well, those two L tetrominoes must be connected somehow, and we only have one more shape to place, so that shape must be the one that connects them. It can't be an I tetromino; that doesn't fit in the available space in the third row, and it isn't quite long enough to connect the two L's if you place it in the second row. The S tetromino can't connect them either.

The L tetromino could make the connection across the third row—but it can't touch other L tetrominoes. That only leaves the T, which can only be placed in one orientation, giving us the answer.

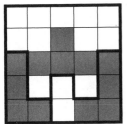

You'll discover even more solving techniques as you go. Happy puzzling!

129 EASY

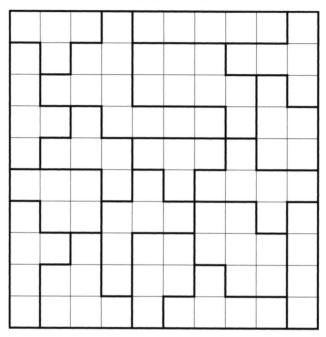

130 EASY

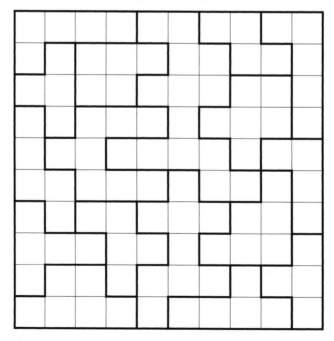

131 EASY

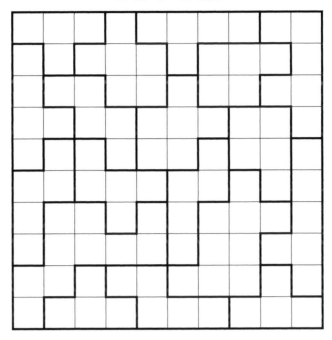

132 EASY

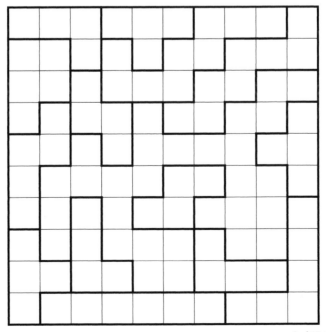

133 EASY

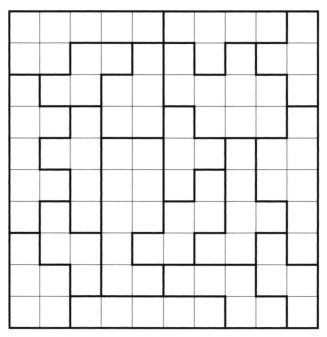

134 EASY

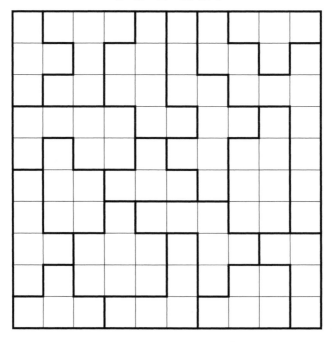

135 EASY

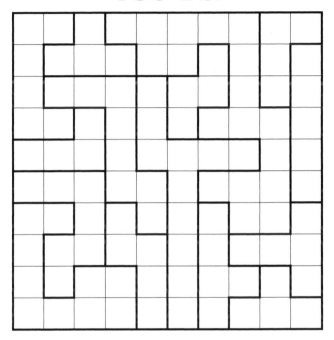

136 EASY

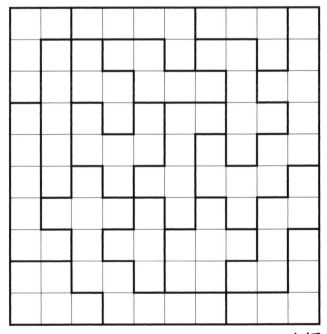

137 EASY

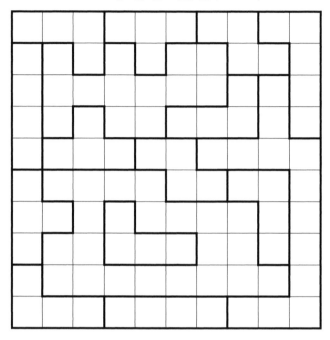

138 EASY

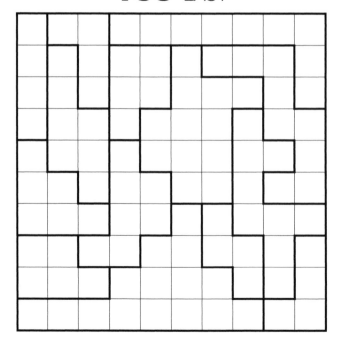

139 EASY

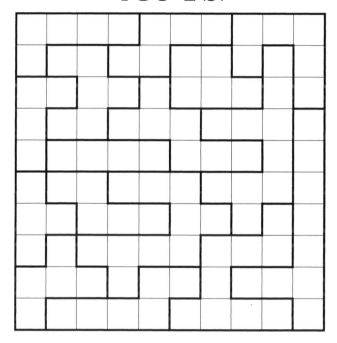

140 EASY

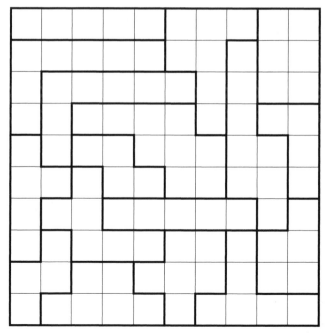

141 MEDIUM

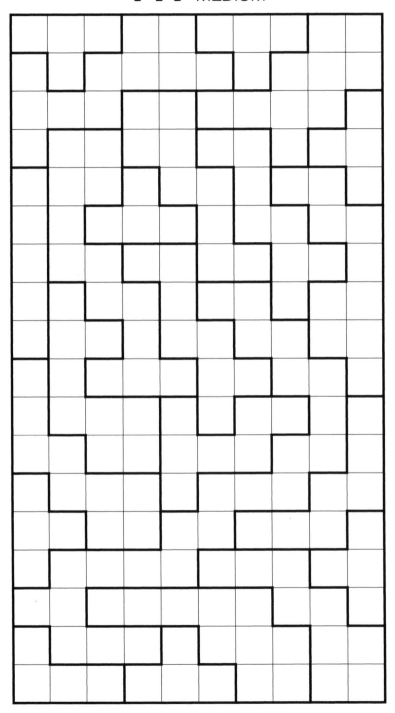

142 MEDIUM

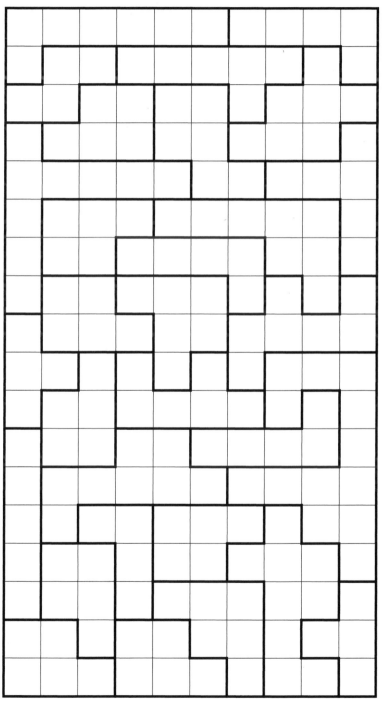

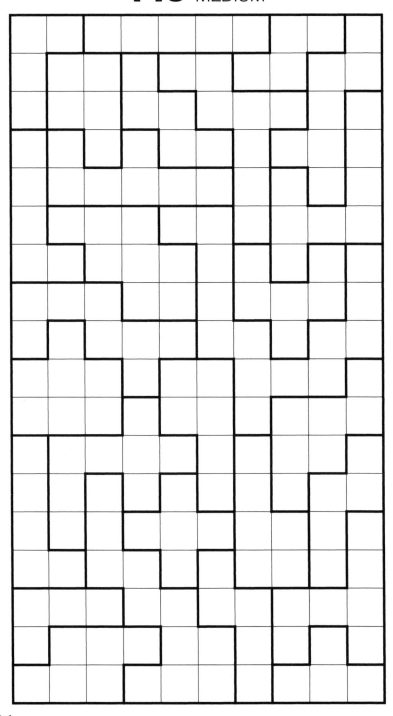

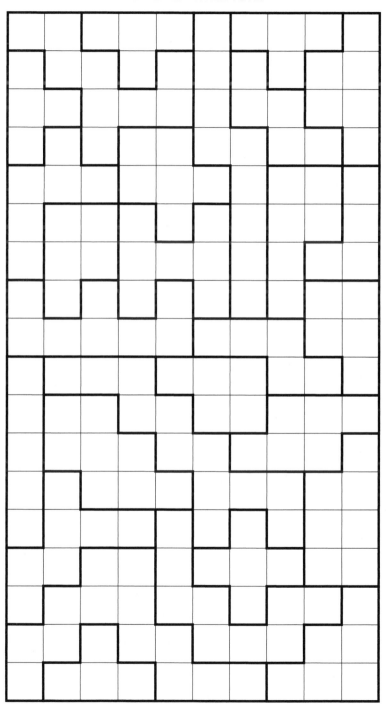

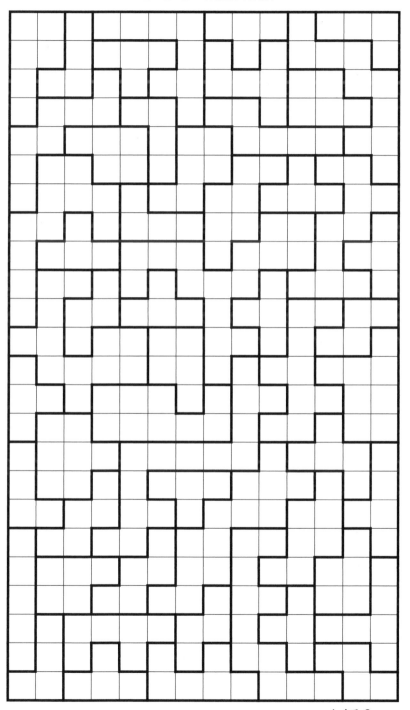

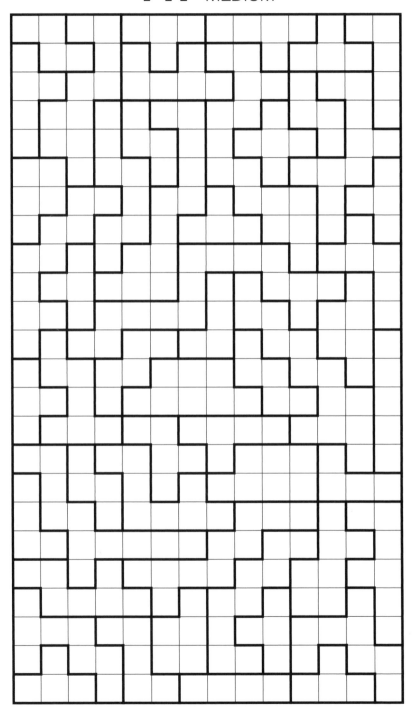

148 HARD

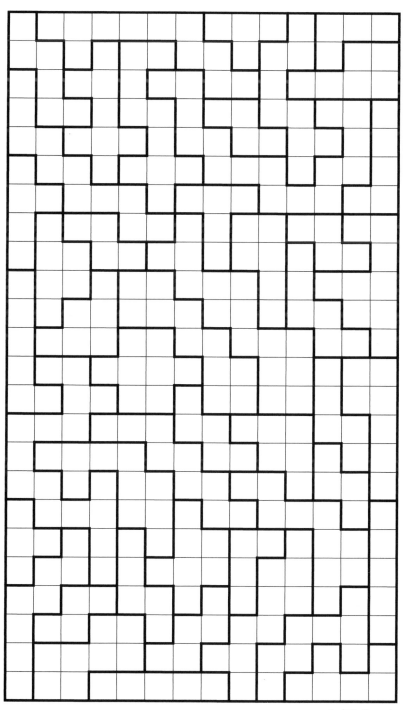

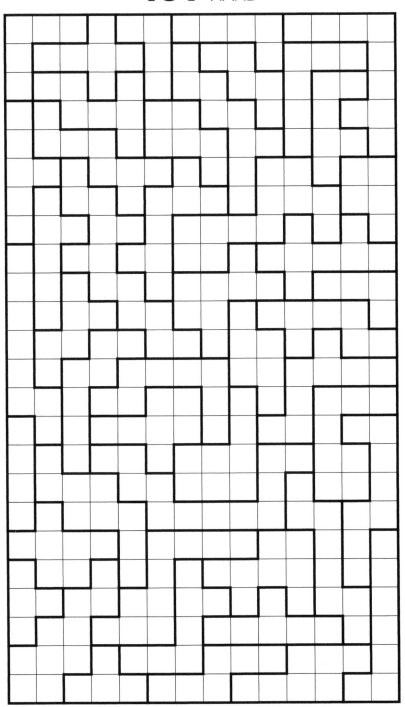

MASYU

Masyu puzzles are like mazes without walls. Your goal is to draw a single unbroken loop in the grid that travels horizontally and vertically, never crosses itself, and passes through every white and black circle. There are, however, some extra rules you must follow. When the line passes through a white circle, it must go straight; the line may never turn on a white circle. Additionally, the line must make at least one 90 degree turn on one side of the white circle or the other. (It may turn in both squares, but it is not required to do so.) When the line passes through a black circle, it must turn; the line may never go straight through a black circle. Additionally, the line may not turn again in either of the squares immediately adjacent to the black circle in the path. The line must go straight for two squares before turning again. Note that the path does not have to pass through every square of the grid.

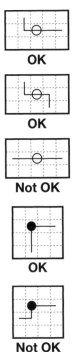

Let's solve a masyu puzzle from beginning to end. From this starting grid, an experienced masyu solver would be able to draw in a number of lines right away. For instance, remember that the path must go straight when it passes through a white circle. That means that

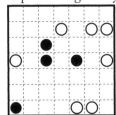

whenever a white circle is next to the edge of the board, the path must travel parallel to the edge of the board as it travels through that circle. When there are multiple white circles near each other along the border, we also learn the points where the line turns. Take a look at the two white circles in the lower right. The line has to turn in one square adjacent to each circle, and of the two squares on either side of each circle, one of them is a white circle where the path is not allowed to turn. Therefore the line must turn in the two empty squares on either side of the two adjacent white circles. Similarly, in the upper right, the path cannot turn in the empty space between the two white circles (since the path is a single loop that doesn't branch off from itself), and must therefore turn in the two squares shown.

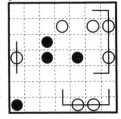

Now let's look at the black circles. The circle in the lower left corner is easy: there are only two directions the line can go, so we can extend the line two squares up from the corner and two squares to the right. (And since we've connected to the line passing through the white circle, we can make a 90 degree turn on the other side of that circle.) Then there are the two vertically adjacent black circles in the third column. Whenever we have two black circles next to each other like this, we can draw a line for each circle that extends directly away from the other circle.

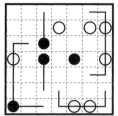

Why? Well, imagine that the path extended down from the topmost of the two circles. The path must go straight for two squares from that circle—but then that means the line would be passing straight through the black circle below it, which breaks the rule that the path must turn when it passes through a black circle. So that leaves three directions that the line can travel, and it can't go both to the left and to the right (or it wouldn't be turning as it goes through the black circle), so one of the directions must be straight up.

Let's see if drawing those lines has given us any more opportunities to make deductions. Aha—the two unused white circles in the second row are each adjacent to a part of the path that's equivalent to being next to a wall, so we can draw lines through them parallel to the existing lines. And take a look at the lower of the two adjacent black circles: the path can't extend from there to the left, because it would intersect the existing line. Therefore, it must extend to the right, reaching the other black circle in that row. What else can we do? Well, there's only one direction the path in the lower right of the grid can go, so let's extend it one square to the left, out of the corner it's in. Same thing with the line extending to the right from the black circle in the lower left corner: it can only go up, connecting with the path above it.

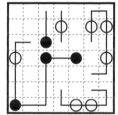

We've got a lot of information now. Take another look at the black circle in the third row. The line can't extend to the right, because the path couldn't go straight for two squares before turning; it would have to turn in the adjacent square. So the line extends to the left, connecting with the path. Follow that path up to the top of the grid. Which direction does it go? It can't go to the left, because that area is blocked off; there's nowhere in that direction to connect with the path. So it turns right instead.

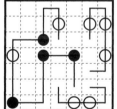

Finally, let's look at the black circle in the fifth column. The line must extend from it either up or down—but if it goes up, we're trapped in a dead end that can't get back to the path. Therefore, we extend the line down two squares instead.

Now we've used all the information provided by the circles: we have lines extending in two directions from each black circle, straight lines through each white circle, and each white circle already has at least one turn in the path in an adjacent square. So all that remains is to connect the line segments we have into a single connected loop. We can start in the middle of the sixth row. There's a dead end above that line segment, so it must turn to the right to connect with the path. That blocks off one of the places the line in the lower right could connect; it goes up to connect instead. Now there are just two endpoints left, and there is only one way to connect them: with a straight line. And we're done!

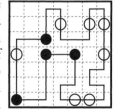

155 EASY

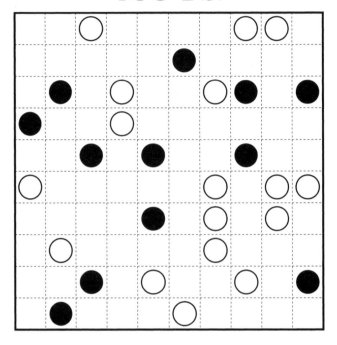

156 EASY

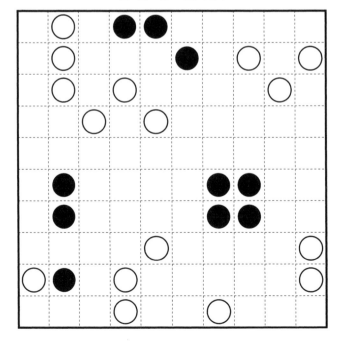

157 EASY

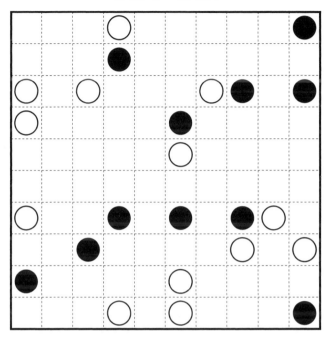

158 EASY

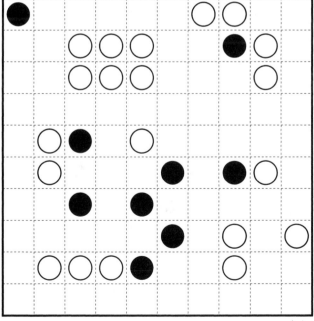

159 EASY

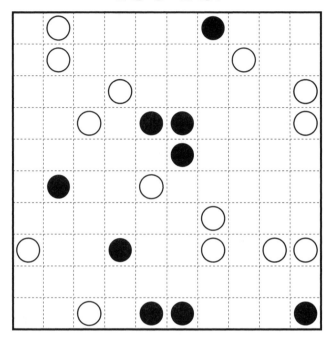

160 EASY

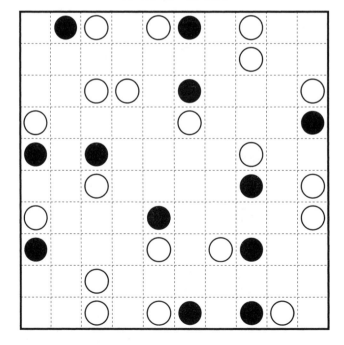

161 EASY

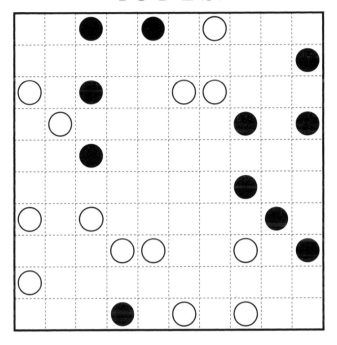

162 EASY

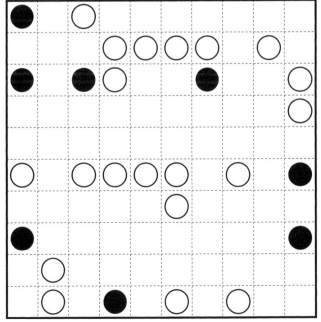

163 EASY

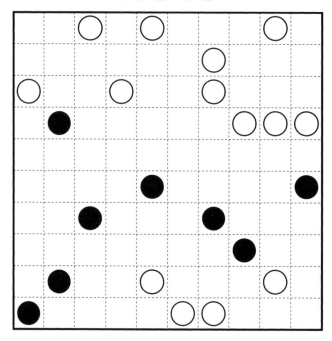

164 EASY

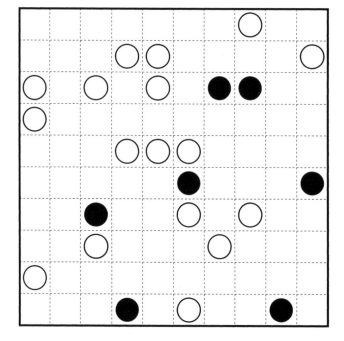

165 EASY

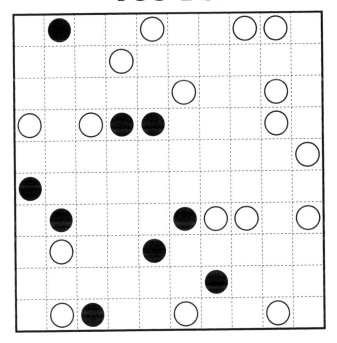

166 EASY

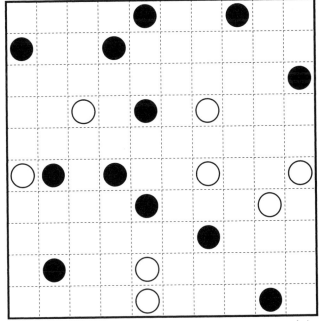

167 MEDIUM

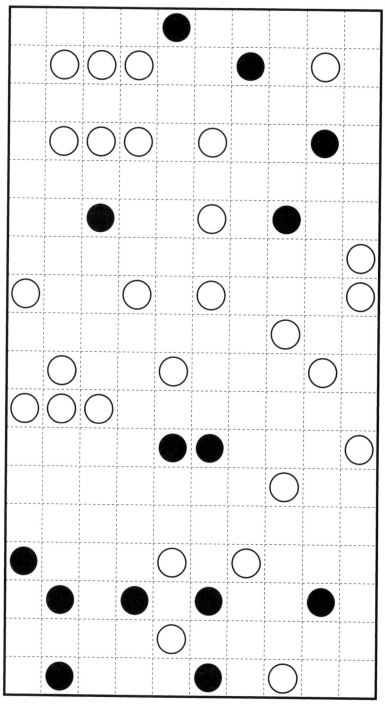

168 MEDIUM

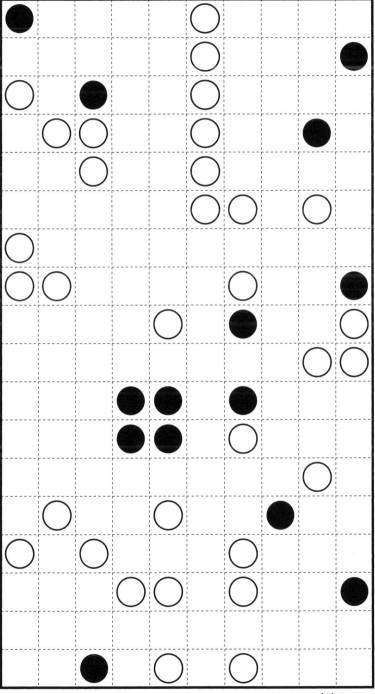

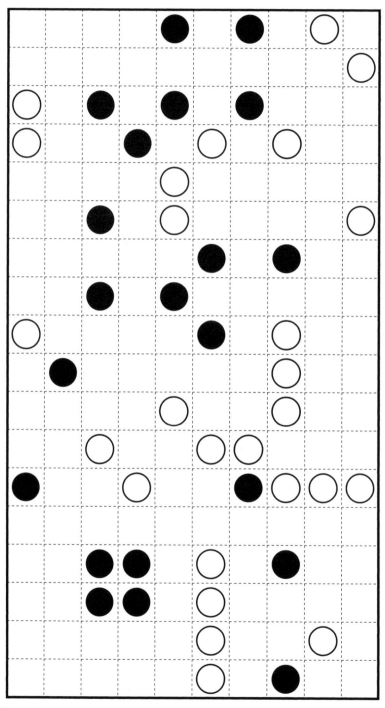

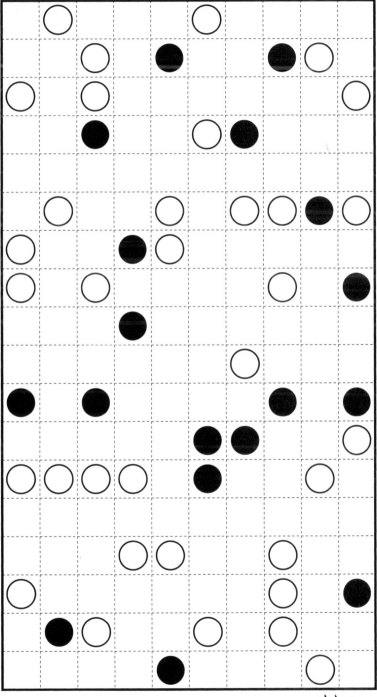

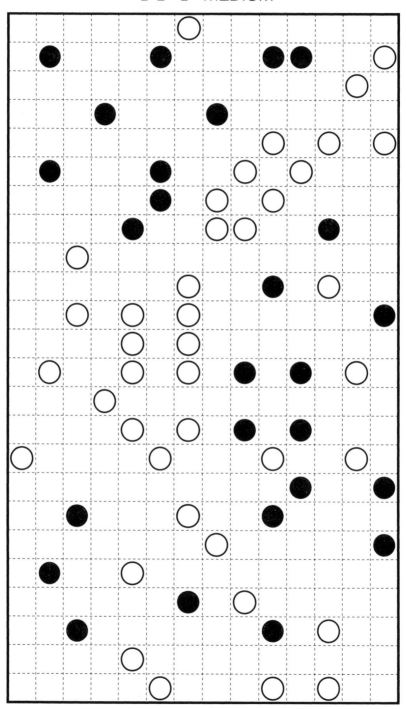

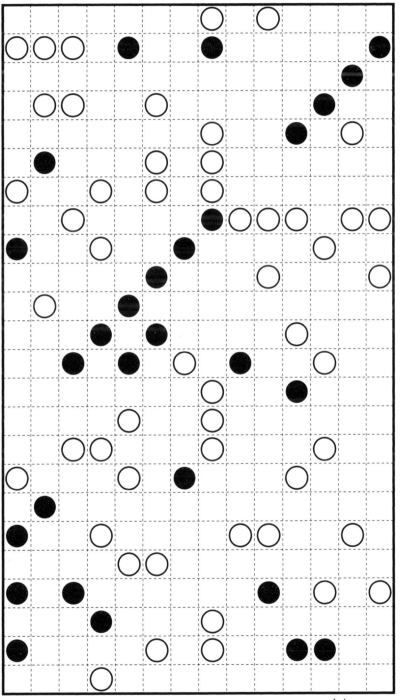

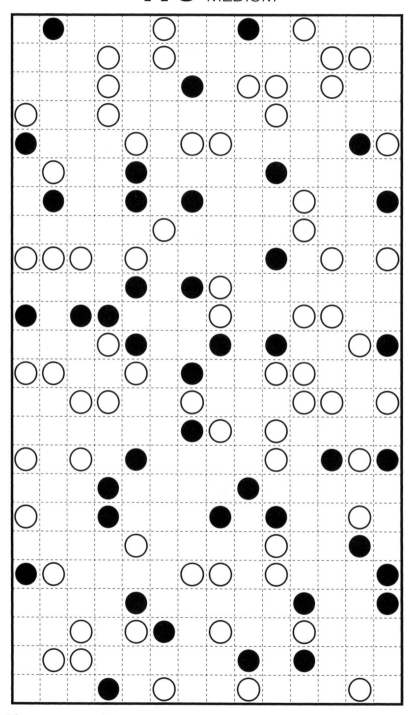

174 HARD

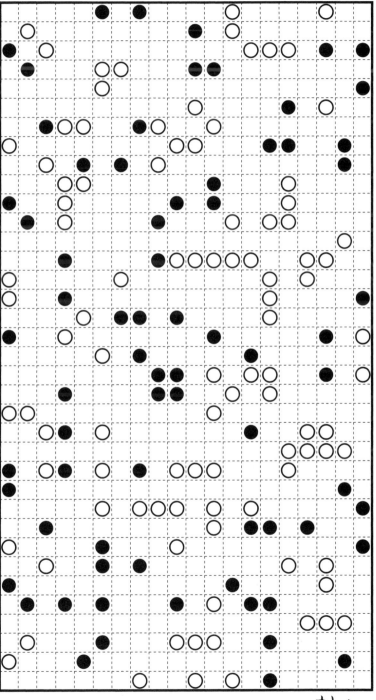

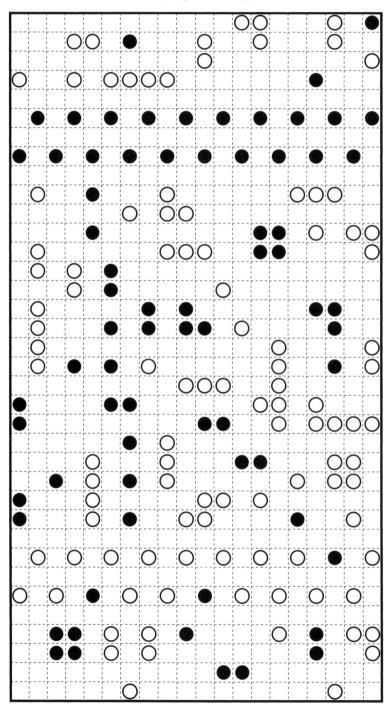

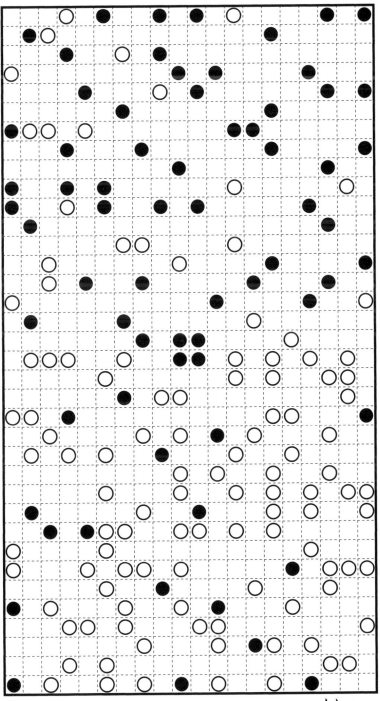

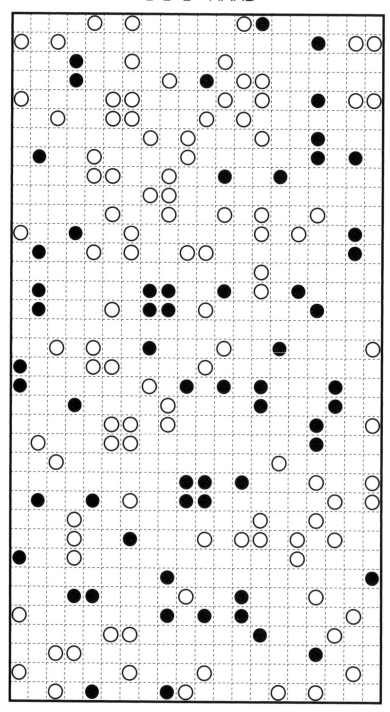

180 HARD

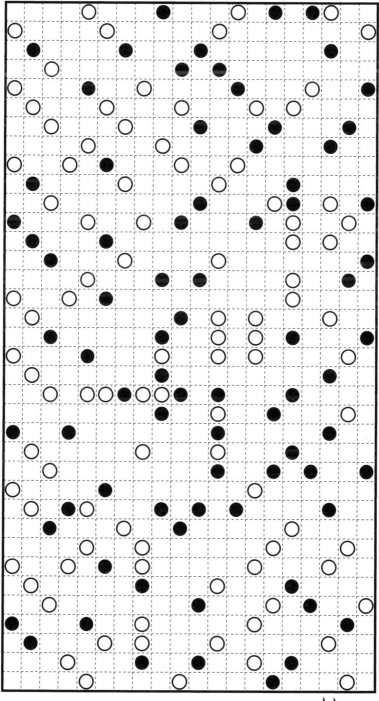

NUMBER LINK

The rules for Number Link puzzles are as simple as can be: connect each pair of matching numbers with a line (moving horizontally and vertically but not diagonally). Lines may not cross each other. The unique solution happens to use every square, though even if we didn't mention that, the puzzle would still have just that one solution.

While the rules may be simple, the puzzles themselves range from easy to very complex, and there are many approaches to use when solving. Let's take a look at a Number Link puzzle together so you can get a feel for the kinds of strategies you might use while solving.

We'll start by looking at that pair of 5's. We could connect them very simply by starting with the 5 in the lower left, moving two squares up and then two squares to the right—but then there's no way for the 1's to connect with each other, because the lower left 1 is then surrounded by lines and other numbers. So how can the 5's connect without blocking the 1's? The path from the 5 can't go around from below, because the 2 and 4 are blocking the path that way; there's a diagonal gap between them, but we can only travel horizontally and vertically. So the path connecting the 5's must somehow go around the 1 in the upper right. Given that, let's figure out the parts of the 1 and 5 paths that we can be sure of. The section of the 5 path that must go around the upper 1 leaves only one direction for the 1 path to begin—straight down—and then that path must go to the left; if it doesn't, there's no way for it to reach the other 1. When that path starts heading to the left, it blocks off one of the directions the 5 path can go, and extending that path in the only available direction gives us a grid that looks like this. (We've added small notes at the ends of the partial 5 path to indicate what it will eventually connect to.)

Now let's turn our attention to the 4 at the top of the grid. The part of the 5 path that we've drawn blocks its path from going down or to the right, so it goes to the left, and turns at the corner. We can see that the general path it takes to connect to the other 4 goes down and to the right, but does it go straight down before reaching the corner, or does it detour along the way? As it happens, it must go straight down; if it veers to the right at all, it'll block the 5's from connecting. The 5 and 1 paths also go straight down, and we now have two pairs connected.

Next, let's take a look at that pair of 2's. We can see that the path starting from the 2 in the lower left must begin by traveling two squares to the right, but does it go up or down from there? If it goes up, the path will block the pair of 3's from connecting, so the path must go down, around the lower 3. As the path from the 2 in the upper right comes down to meet it, the path from the 5 must continue extending down next to it, giving us the nearly solved grid shown at left.

At this point there are so few squares left, it's a simple matter to make the last two connections. And we're done!

158

181 EASY

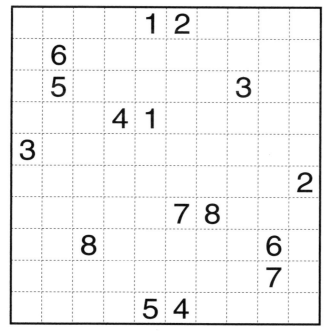

182 EASY

183 EASY

1								3
		6						
	4				7	8		
			5					
						2		
			8					
						2		
			6	1				4
						3		
7								5

184 EASY

5								
			2		5	6	7	
			1					
			4					
			3					
					8			
					6			
					7			
	1	2	3		4			
								8

185 EASY

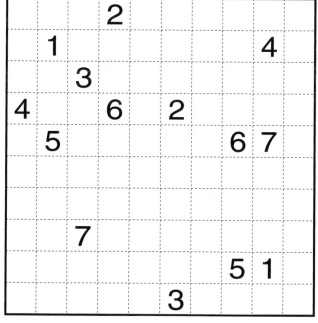

186 EASY

187 EASY

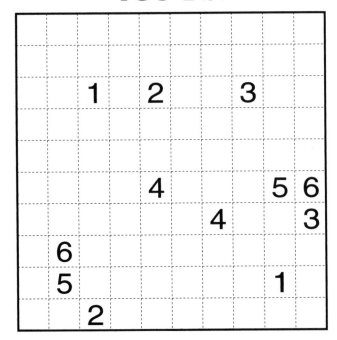

188 EASY

189 EASY

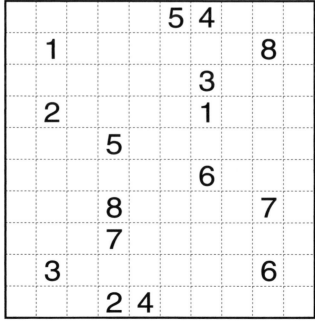

190 EASY

191 EASY

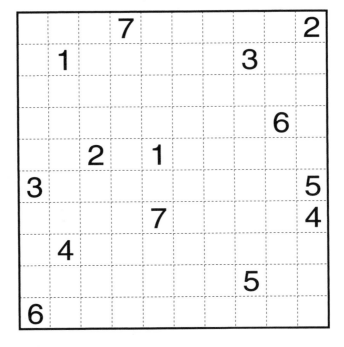

192 EASY

193 MEDIUM

194 MEDIUM

			1						
	3				2				
							4		
			4	5			1		
								6	
				3					
2								7	
								8	
	9								
					10				
		7					9		
				11				5	
		8							
	10							11	
				6					

195 MEDIUM

1							2
	6		9		10		
					7		
					9		
			1				
							11
				8			
				11			10
		5			2	3	
					8		
					7		4
					6		
					5		
4							3

197 MEDIUM

							5					9	
		6	9									19	
										10			
									20				
					20						19		
							16						
						15							
						21							
	5	1	2	6					15	11	12	16	
	3			3					13			12	
	4			4					14			11	
	7	1	2	8					17	14	13	18	
				21									
						22							
									17				
		7		8			22						
18													
													10

198 MEDIUM

1	2												
		3	4								4		
				5	6							6	
												12	
						7	8						
								9	10				
								13					
										8			
		5											
3	16												
		7	10						9				
									12				
		14							14				
	11					11			13				
		1								15	2		
												16	15

199 MEDIUM

						1	2				
								3	4	5	
		4	11	5							
								18	8	12	
1	15				15	2					
				19	17						
	6	7				3					
			14					8	9		
			13	14							
			18	7					16	20	
16	17	6									
					10	11	12				
	13	9	10								
			19	20							

201 HARD

202 HARD

203 HARD

204 HARD

205 HARD

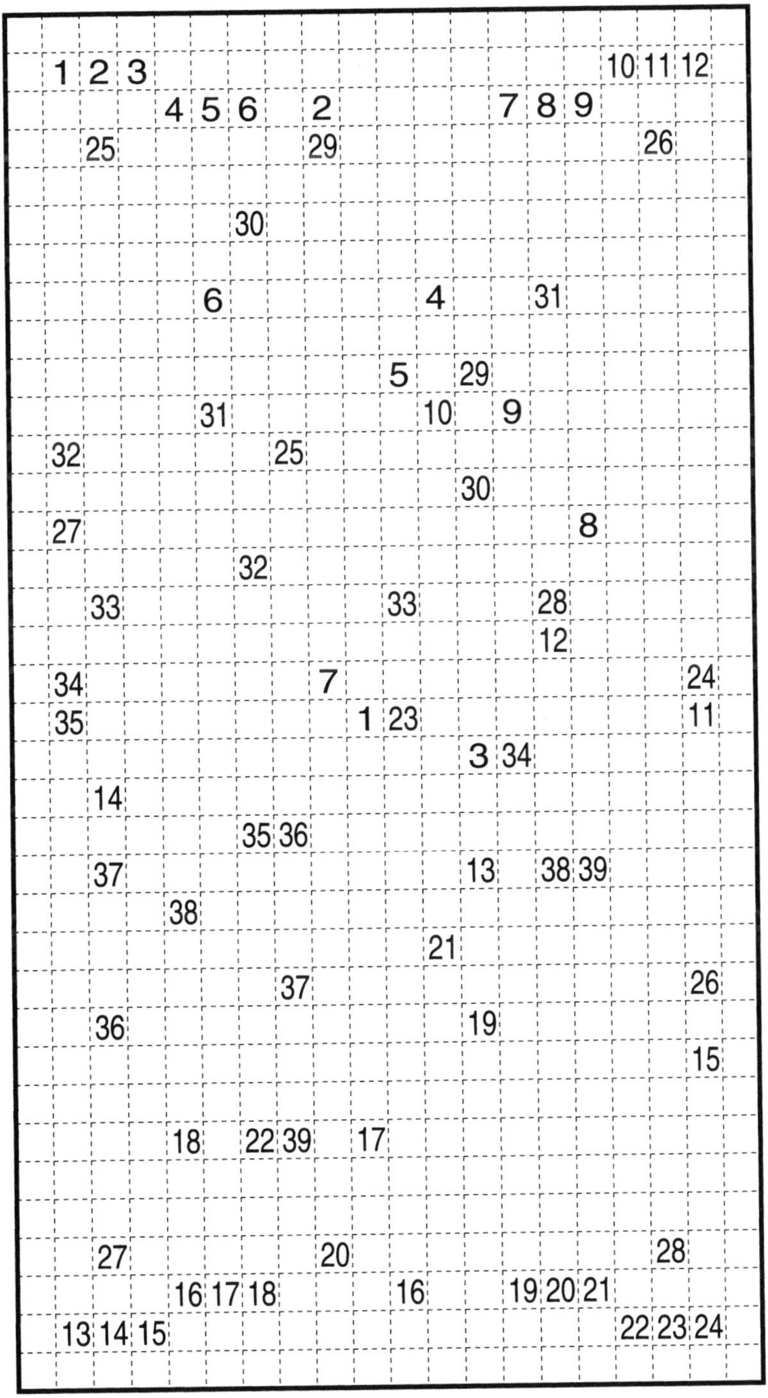
1 2 3 10 11 12
4 5 6 2 7 8 9
25 29 26
30
6 4 31
5 29
31 10 9
32 25
30
27 8
32
33 33 28
12
34 7 24
35 1 23 11
3 34
14
35 36
37 13 38 39
38
21
37 26
36 19
15
18 22 39 17
27 20 28
16 17 18 16 19 20 21
13 14 15 22 23 24

206 HARD

NURIKABE

In a nurikabe puzzle, the grid is to be shaded in so that it contains a connected "river" of black squares. The river surrounds many islands of white squares; each number in the grid is part of a different island, every island has a number, and the number indicates how many white squares that island contains. Also, no 2×2 square in the grid may be colored entirely black. That's it! But of course, those simple rules lead to an endless variety of logical possibilities.

Here's a small nurikabe puzzle as an example. The first thing we can do is shade in any squares that are adjacent to two numbers, because each number is part of its own island, and no island will ever contain more than one number.

The next thing to remember is that all the black squares in the grid must be connected into one big river. So any black square that's surrounded on all sides but one by white squares must extend out in the one available direction. Similarly, any numbered square (other than a 1) that's surrounded on all sides but one by black squares must also continue in the direction available to it. There are three black squares that we can extend out by one square (giving you the grid at left), and three numbered squares that we can do the same with. (Dots indicate squares that we know must be white.) After adding a dot below the 5 in the upper left corner, there is still only one square into which that island can continue, so we can add a second dot below the first one. We can add one dot to the left of the 3 in the sixth row, and from the 4 in the bottom row, we can extend all the way around the corner, which accounts for all four of the squares in that island, so we can shade in the next square to close off that island.

What now? Well, the block of two black squares in the lower right of the grid is all but surrounded by white squares. Since there's only one available square for it to extend into, we can shade that square in. Along the left side of the grid, the island with the 5 has extended far enough that there's only one square between it and the 2. Those are separate islands, so we can color the square between them black. And notice

179

the island with the 3 that has two of its squares accounted for. The third square of the island must either extend upward or to the left. In either case, the second square of the fifth row must be black (because islands are surrounded by black squares, and also because of the nearby 2). Now the grid looks like this.

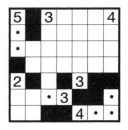

There's now only one direction in which the island with the 2 can extend, so draw a dot below the 2 and shade in the surrounding squares. That leaves the second square in the bottom row surrounded by black squares, which means it can't be part of any island, so shade that square in as well. With those squares colored in, there's only one square into which the nearby 3 island can extend, so add a dot in that square and shade in

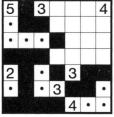

the square above it to close off the island. And the black square above the 2 must extend to the right to connect with the other black squares, which forces the 5 island to extend two more squares to the right, after which we can surround that island with more black squares since it's now reached the correct size of five squares.

We're getting close to finishing now. The L-shaped group of black squares in the upper left has only one outlet into which it can extend, so we can shade that square in, which forces the nearby 3 island to extend two squares to the right, after which the surrounding squares can be shaded. Let's look at the grid again to see how it's coming along.

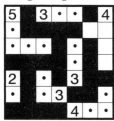

Notice the fifth square in the third row. That square can't be black, or we'd have a 2×2 square that was all black, which is against the rules. So it must be white. What island is that square part of? Not the one with the 4, because it's too far away; for it to reach the 4, the island would have to be at least five squares long. So it's part of the island with the 3 instead, and we can draw a dot in the square between it and the 3, and shade in the surrounding squares.

Finally, the black square in the top row must extend to the square below it to connect to the rest of the river of black squares, which leaves exactly enough available squares for the island with the 4. And we're done!

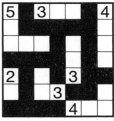

207 EASY

4				1				3	
	1					1			
			2				4		
	3								1
					3				
4			3				1		
									4
	3				5				

208 EASY

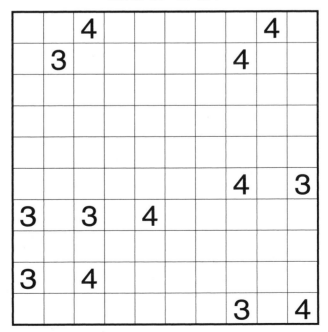

		4					4		
	3					4			
						4		3	
3		3		4					
3		4							
							3		4

209 EASY

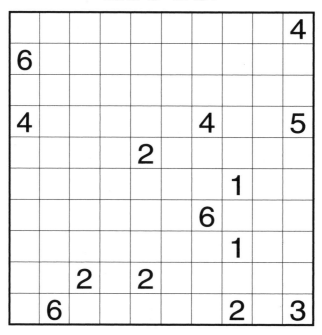

								4
6								
4					4			5
			2					
						1		
					6			
						1		
	2		2					
	6						2	3

210 EASY

					4		
	1		1				
		3					
3				1			
			1		3		4
	2			1		1	
			2				
						4	
							1
3	2			4			

211 EASY

17		4			5			
					5			
				3				
3								
				2		4		
	1							

212 EASY

3				4		4			
4									
					2				3
							2		
			4						
3					3				
									3
				4		3			5

Nurikabe ぬりかべ 183

213 EASY

	3		3			3			
	3				3			
	3			3				3
			3					
						3		
					3			
						1		3
	3		3					

214 EASY

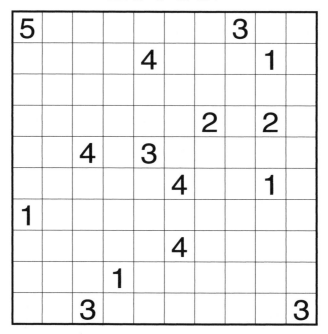

5						3		
			4				1	
					2		2	
	4		3					
				4			1	
1								
				4				
		1						
	3							3

215 EASY

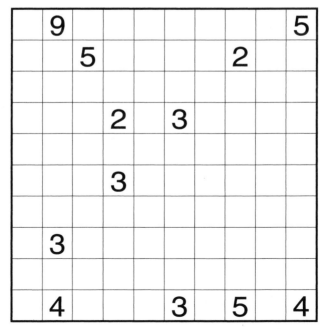

		6			2			3			
			1							4	
				2		5					
		2									
						2					
		3			3						
		2		2			2	4			

216 EASY

	9						5
	5				2		
		2	3				
		3					
3							
4			3	5	4		

217 EASY

			4					5
			4					1
			6					4
1					5			
3					2			
5					8			

218 EASY

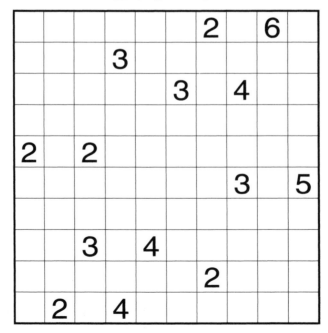

					2		6	
		3						
				3		4		
2		2						
						3		5
		3		4				
					2			
	2		4					

8		6				4	
							1
			1		6		
							2
							3
							4
7					1		
		7		3			
		3					
			2		5		3
		2					
	1		3				
4				1		2	4

						2	
2		5	1		3		
						2	
	3						
						2	
	2						
		5		5	1		2
	3						
						2	
	1						
						2	
2		3	2		6		
						1	
	4						
						1	
	1						
		1		3	2		2
	3						

221 MEDIUM

4					4				
			6						
							5		
				1					
			5		3				
	4			1					
			4		2				
									5
			4						
									5
					7		3		
		5							
4		3				4			
									1

		3					
	3			2			3
	5						3
					6	1	
			4				
		3		4			
3							
				3	5		
		4					
1				4			
		3					
	2						
				5		3	
							3
3		2					

223 MEDIUM

4		3		3								1	
						5							
													3
			2				1						
	3				2				6				
			4								1		
						3							
								1			4		
			3				2						
										7			
4													
		5						4					1
					6					3			
						4							1
				2							2		
6								2					
											3		
			3				6		3				
		1			1			5					
			2										
										1			
						1					4		
				3									
3			4				3			5			

Nurikabe ぬりかべ 191

224 MEDIUM

225 MEDIUM

5	9				1		6		
	7						3		
				9		3			
3	4					8			
6			3					2	
			6		1			2	6
10	6			2		5			
	4					4			1
			3					7	3
			6		5				
			4					2	
			3		5			3	1

					4				
				7					
5			1			5			
	2								
		3			1			1	
			3			3			6
	2			6			2		
			2			2		3	
	2								
			3			2			2
1		2			2			3	
			2			2		3	
	5			5			5		5
			5						
2					5				
							5		
	5								
			5						
			3			6			
	4				5				

		6				4	3	
				5				
							6	3
					2			
	2		4					
								5
	5		3			4		
				2				
		1						
	4			3				
3		4						2
						3		
		2		1		4		
1			2				2	
	3						3	
2		2		5				
						4		
		3				4		
	4						4	
		2						
3				3				3
	4			4				
						4	2	

228 HARD

9									
				10					1
		3							
					9				
								3	
							5		
2		4						3	
				1					
3		5			4				
							4		
		8							
			7						
								25	
		4				1			
							3		
		3							
						2			
				4					4
		7							
	5				4				
			4						

2	2				5	2	5
		1					
			5				
		2					
	5				2		
1				2		2	2
		2		2	5		
1							
5			1		5	1	
		5					1
				2			
2							
		2			1		1
	1						
		5		5	2		
	5		2				5
		2		2	2		
	2		1				
2		5		2			5
		2				1	
					5		
	2			5	2		

10	8	2					2	1					
				3					2				
											2		
					3								
							6	2				10	
						5				5			
2				5									4
	6	4				1						3	
								6					
						2				5			
		2			3							8	
							2						
		2						3					4
	7			5					13				
						9							
5										3			1
		1						5					
					4					4			
6		2						7					
							3						
			3						5			2	
2					4					5			
						4							
	2							1			3		
		1					4						
				12									
	2						4			6		6	
3									3				10
		3					3						
4				5	3								
								4					
		4											
			1						1				
					3	5				2		4	1

231 HARD

1	2	3	4	5	6	7	8	9	10	11
3		1					4		4	
						2		4		
	1			1					5	
			8				2			
3			3			2				
	2									
3		5				1		2		
				6						4
	1		3				1			
1			1			8				
4					4				1	
		3				7				
	5				2			1		
7										
									17	
	2		2							
		4								
	3		1	5			3		16	
			4		4					
		3					1		8	
2					3					
	3		2	4					7	
		2		3		2		1		
									10	
			3							
	5	2								
6					8					
	6		6			3				
					1					
					6	6			4	
	3		1			1				5
		1			1			3		
		4	1							
6					3				6	9

232 HARD

RIPPLE EFFECT

In a ripple effect puzzle, the grid is divided into many smaller areas by dark lines. The areas are different sizes, and do not contain any repeated numbers. An area with one square will contain only the number 1; an area with two squares will contain the numbers 1 and 2, an area with six squares will contain the number 1 through 6; and so forth. Numbers may be repeated within a row or column, but they must be separated by at least a number of cells equal to that number—so each number placed by the solver sends out ripples that affect where other numbers can go.

Let's take a look at an easy ripple effect puzzle and see how to solve it. The first thing you can do is to look for areas that have only a single square in them; you can fill those areas in with a 1 right away. There are three of them: two in the upper left and one in the lower right. The two in the upper left are each adjacent to the same 1×3 area. One of the three squares in it must contain a 1, but it can't be either of the squares adjacent to the 1s we just wrote in, so it must be the bottom square. As for the bottom right, there are two areas we can make deductions in. The 1×2 area above the 1 contains a 1 and a 2. The square directly above the 1 isn't another 1, so it's the 2 and the other square contains the 1. Then there's the L-shaped three-square area in the corner, which contains a 1, 2, and 3. The lower left square in that area can't contain a 1, and it can't contain a 2 either (since there is only one square between it and the 2 above it, and there must be at least two squares between 2s), so it's a 3. The 1 can't go directly to the right of the adjacent 1, so it goes in the corner and the remaining square contains a 2. Let's check in on the grid and see how it looks.

That 3 in the lower right looks like we can use it to place some more numbers. The L-shaped four-square area to its left must contain a 3, but none of the bottom three squares is far enough away from the 3 that's already there, so it must go in the single top square. Looking at the 2×2 above that, we can see there's only one place for a 3 to be placed in it (in the lower left), and also only one place in the four-square L to the left (at the top). What about the five-square shape just above the L and the square? There must be a 3 in it, but all three columns have a 3 in it already. That's all right, though—we can place a 3 in the upper right, because there are three squares between it and the 3 below it in the same column. While we're in that area, let's place a 2 in the only space left available for it (the lower left), and check in on the grid.

From here we can place many more 3s: on the right side of the grid, in the lower left square of the top L, and the lower right corner of the L below it; and in the vertical 1×3 area in the second column, in the middle square. A 2 must go above that, which forces the 2 in the upper left L to go in the top left corner. (And the 1 must go to its right, and the 3 below it.) Now let's look at the 1×5 rectangle at the top of the grid. What can go in its leftmost square? There's a 1 below and directly adjacent to it, a 2 separated from it by one square, a 3 separated by two squares, and a 4 separated by 3 squares. Therefore it can't be a 1, 2, 3, or 4, and must be a 5. We can also place a 3 in that area (in the second square), but that's all we can do there for now. Let's move down from there to the L shape with the 3 and 4 already filled in. The lower right square can't be a 2 (because of the 2 too close above it), so it's a 1, and the 2 is to its left. In the 2×2 square, the upper right square isn't a 1, so it's a 4, and the square below it is a 1.

The grid's starting to fill up. In the L on the bottom of the grid, we can see that the 4 can only be in the center square of the three empty squares. The square to its left can't be a 2, so it's the 1, and the 2 is on the right. Now, going back to the five-square area above it, which has the 1, 2, and 3 filled in, which square contains the 4 and which the 5? Whichever one has the 4 must have at least four squares between it and the 4 in the same column (on the bottom row of the grid), so the 4 must be in the top square, with the 5 below it. It's easy to finish off the remaining small shapes, so let's take care of those. On the right side of the grid, the lower of the two remaining L shapes can't have a 2 in the lower left, so it's got a 1 there and a 2 in the upper right. The L above it therefore must have its 2 in the upper left and a 1 in the upper right. And the 1 and 2 in the 1×2 area in the lower left are a breeze: 1 on top, 2 below it. Let's take one last look at the grid before finishing this puzzle off.

Almost done—just two areas left! The top area's already partly filled in, so let's take care of it first. The numbers 1, 2, and 4 are left to fill in; the 2 can't go in either of the two squares on the right, so it's in the leftmost empty square. The 1 can't go on the far right either, so that square is the 4, with the 1 to its left. Now let's look at the last area, in the lower left. What can the single square sticking out to the right be? Not a 1 or 2 (too close above and below it), and not a 3 or 4 either (too close to the right). It must be the 5. And what about the top square? The 1, 3, and 4 to its right are all too close, so it can't be any of those; it must be a 2. And where can the 4 go? There are 4s in the same rows as the top and bottom empty squares, separated by one square and two squares, respectively. So those squares are no good, and the 4 goes in the empty square between them. That just leaves 1 and 3, which are easy to place; the top square is too close to the 3 to its right, so the 1 is there, with the 3 at the bottom—and that's it!

First grid:

		1		3		
1		2		1		
	1	3	2			
		4	3		2	1
			3	1	2	
			3		1	

Second grid:

2	1	5	3			
3	2	1	4	3	2	1
1	3	2	5	1	3	2
	1	3	2	4	1	3
		4	3	1	2	1
	1	2	1	3	1	2
	2	1	4	2	3	1

Third grid:

2	1	5	3	2	1	4
3	2	1	4	3	2	1
1	3	2	5	1	3	2
2	1	3	2	4	1	3
1	5	4	3	1	2	1
4	1	2	1	3	1	2
3	2	1	4	2	3	1

233 EASY

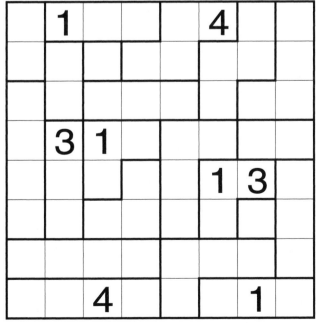

234 EASY

Ripple Effect　波及効果　203

235 EASY

		4		1			
				4			
3						1	
		3				4	
	5				3		
	3						4
			3				
			4		1		

236 EASY

3						3	2
4							
			1	2			
			4	3			
							4
4	1						3

204

237 EASY

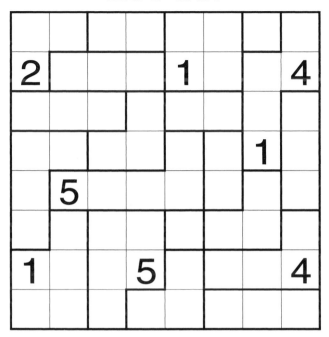

238 EASY

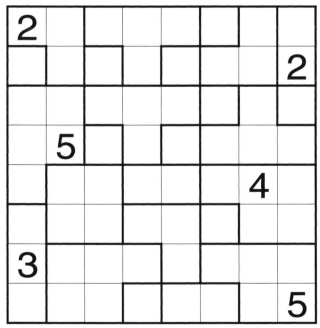

239 EASY

				1			6
			2		4	3	
		2				2	
	2						3
2						6	
	3				3		
	2	1		1			
3			1				

240 EASY

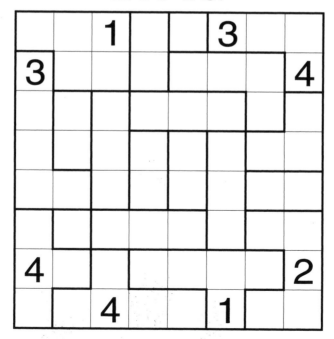

		1			3		
3							4
4							2
		4			1		

241 EASY

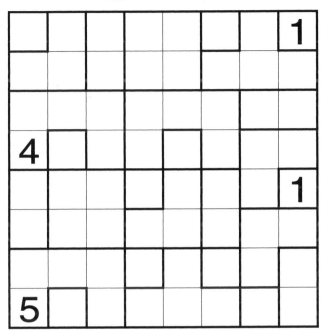

242 EASY

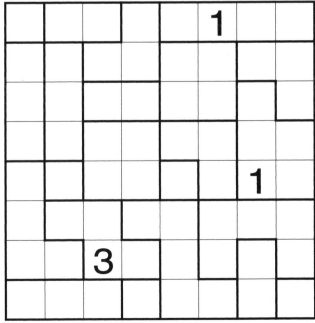

243 EASY

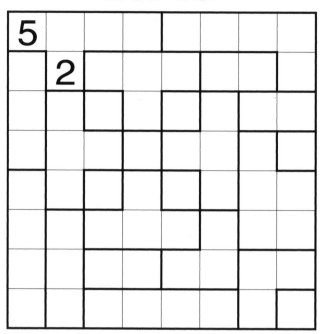

244 EASY

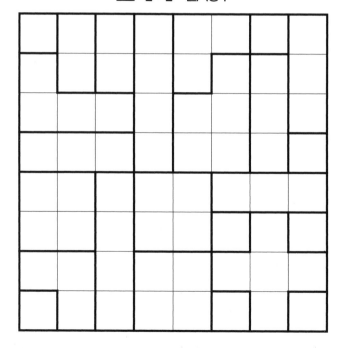

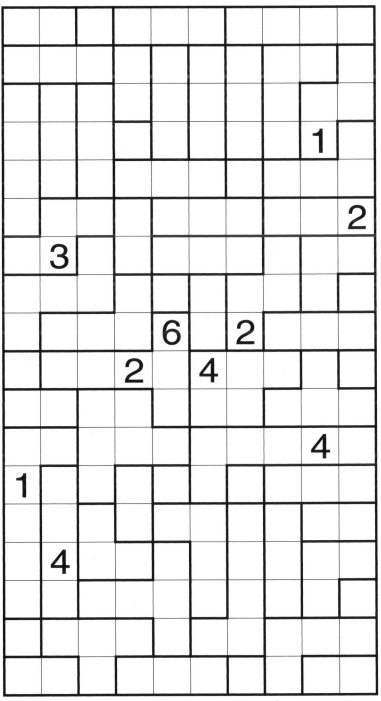

246 MEDIUM

247 MEDIUM

248 MEDIUM

2				7	4	3			
			8	6			2		
	5				2		7		6
				1					5
1		2		3	8	7	4		
4			3						
	7		6						2
		4							4
1			7	5	1		6		
			3		2			2	8
7		6						4	
3			2				4		
	2			4			8		
4	1				5				
5			6	7			5		3
		5	4		6	7			

249 MEDIUM

			3					1
		2		4				
2					6			1
	2		5			1		2
		2		1			5		2
			4					4	
	5			1				1
	1			3		5	1	
		5	6		3			1
2				1			4	
	7				6			
6		4			3		2	
	2		5			2		3
2			1					1
				7		2		
1					2			

Ripple Effect 波及效果 213

250 MEDIUM

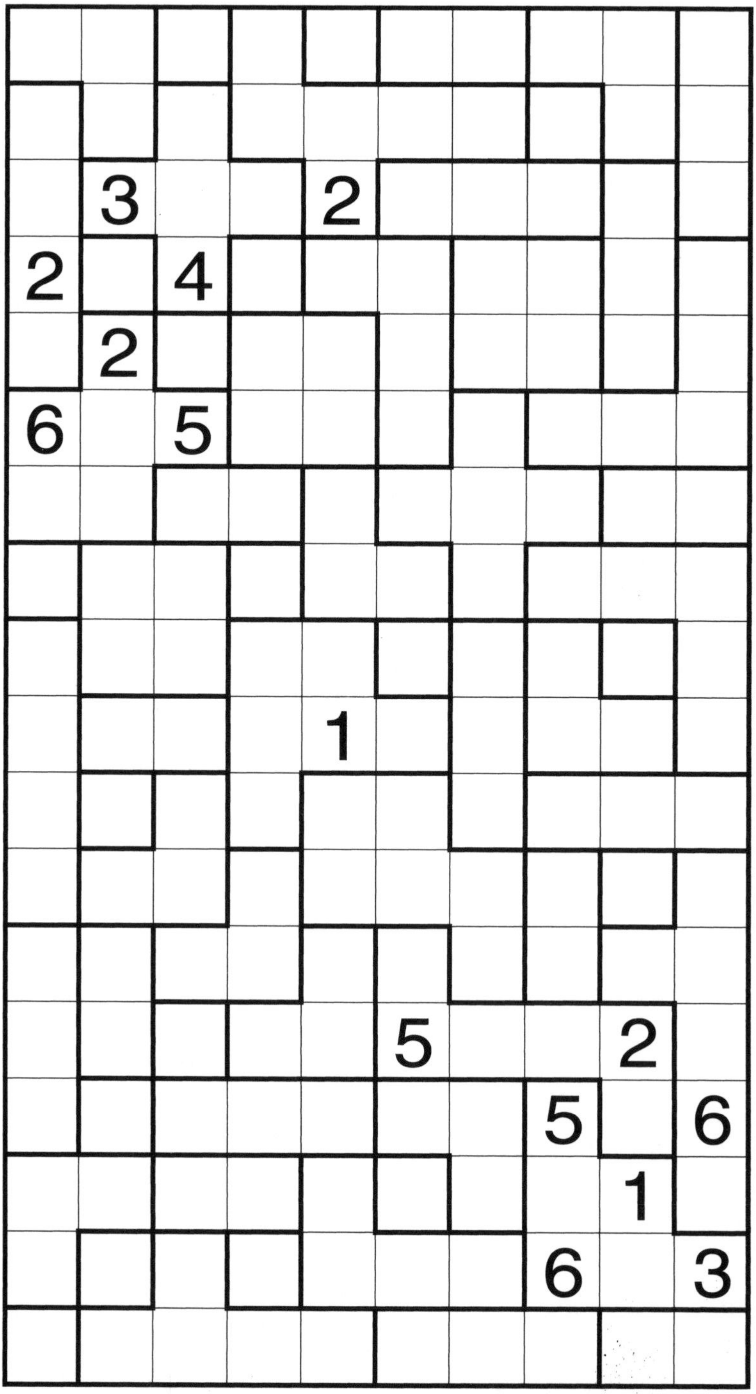

251 MEDIUM

1				4				5	
		3			6				
3		1			1		2		
2		1			1		4		
		3			5				
3				2				1	
		5				2			
			1				2		
	3				1				4
			3				4		
	5		1				2		1
	3		4				1		3
			2				5		
	2				5				4

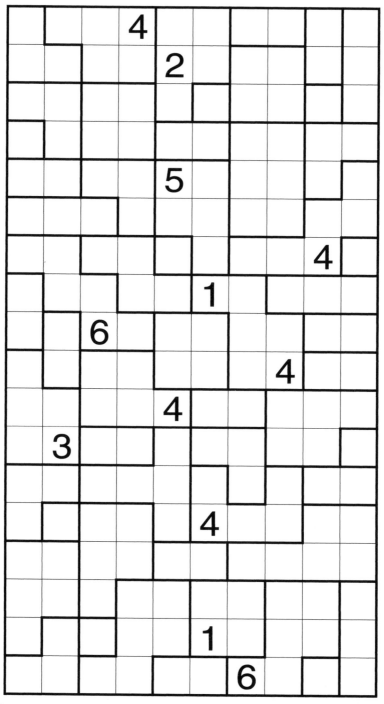

253 HARD

254 HARD

5				2	3				1
		3					1		
4									3
		1		4	3		5		
2			3			1			6
		3					6		
		1					2		
2			2			2			4
		4		2	3		5		
5									1
		2					3		
3				5	3				6

255 HARD

256 HARD

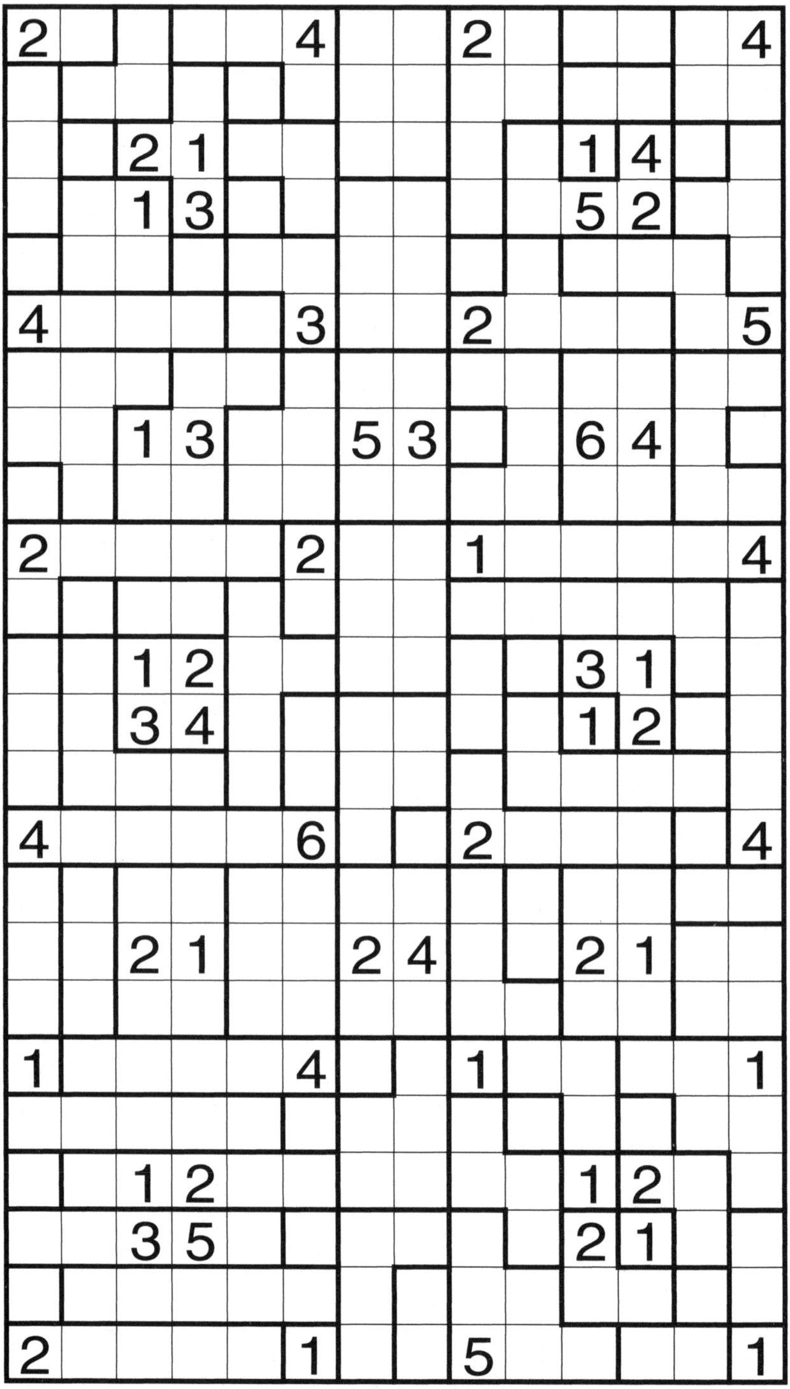

257 HARD

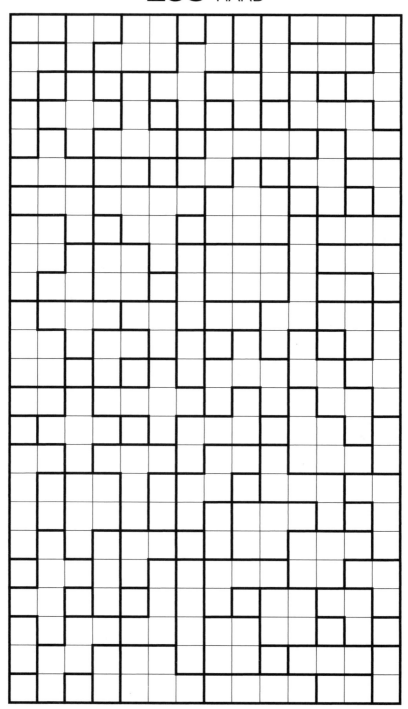

SHIKAKU

The goal in a shikaku puzzle is to divide the grid up into rectangles. Numbers in the grid indicate the size of the area of the rectangle that contains that number. So, for instance, the number 20 might indicate a 1×20, 2×10, or 4×5 rectangle. Each rectangle contains exactly one number, and every square in the grid will be used in exactly one rectangle. The number may appear anywhere inside the rectangle—an edge, a corner, or somewhere in the interior.

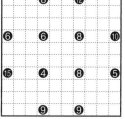

Let's solve a small shikaku puzzle together so you can see how it works.

In this puzzle, there aren't any places where we can draw an entire rectangle right away, but there are a number of deductions we can make to get started. Take a look at the 5 on the right edge of the grid. There's only one shape of rectangle that has an area of 5 squares: 1×5. There's no room for that rectangle to fit horizontally, so it must go vertically. There are six empty squares available in which to fit that rectangle (between the bottom of the grid and the 10 above

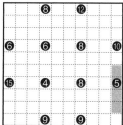

the 5, which is part of a different rectangle), so there are two ways we could fit a 1×5 rectangle there, and we don't know which just yet. But in either case, the rectangle must include the central four squares. We've indicated this with a shaded rectangle, but of course you can notate it in whatever manner you like when you're solving.

What about the 12 on the top row? It's obviously not 1×12 (since the grid is only 10×10), but it could be 2×6 or 3×4—no way for us to tell which right now. Let's look at the 10 above the shaded area instead.

It must be part of a 1×10 or 2×5 rectangle, and there's no room around it to fit a 1×10, so it's 2×5. With the shaded area assigned to the 5, there's now only one place that 2×5 rectangle can go (and that blocks off one of the empty squares next to the shaded area, which means we can complete the rectangle for the 5).

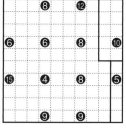

As it happens, locating the rectangle for the 10 also resolves the ambiguity of what size rectangle the 12 is part of: it must be 3×4 (and there's only one place for it to go). Now let's move into the lower left

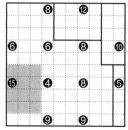

area and look at the 15. It's impossible for it to be part of a 1×15 rectangle, so it'll be a 3×5. There are two ways to fit a 3×5 rectangle in that area, but just as we did earlier, we can indicate the area where the possibilities overlap as definitely being part of the rectangle.

How can we determine which placement of the 3×5 rectangle is correct? Well, let's think about the square in the lower left corner of the grid. It must be part of some rectangle or other—but which? If it's not part of the rectangle belonging to the 15, it must be part of the rectangle that belongs to the lower left 9. However, there's no way to make a 9-square rectangle that includes the corner square and that 9; the largest rectangle you can make in that space is a 1×6. (The other 9 is part of a different rectangle; remember, only one number per rectangle.) Since that's impossible, that square must be part of the 15, and we can draw in that rectangle. While we're at it, let's draw in the rectangle for that 9, since there's now only one possibility (a 3×3 square, with only one place to put it).

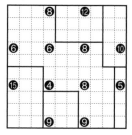

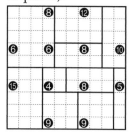

The possibilities for the remaining numbers have narrowed down a lot. The remaining 9 on the bottom row is part of a 3×3 square, and the 8 above it is part of a 2×4 rectangle, which must be placed as far to the right as it can go, otherwise there's no room for the 4 to the left (which must be part of a 2×2 square). The 8 in the middle of the grid has only one possibility as well.

Almost done now! The 8 that remains in the upper left is part of another 2×4 rectangle, leaving two 6s in a 3×4 area. There are multiple ways to draw a 2×3 rectangle for either one of the 6s, but only one way to fit two 2×3 rectangles in that area—with a vertical line down the center. And we're done!

259 EASY

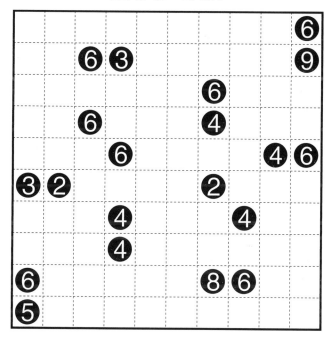

260 EASY

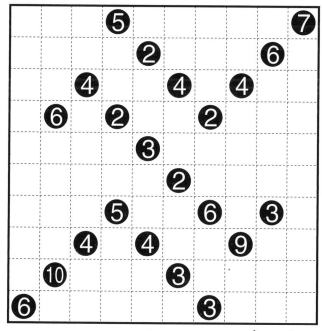

Shikaku　四角に切れ　225

261 EASY

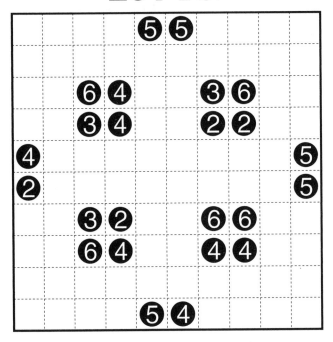

262 EASY

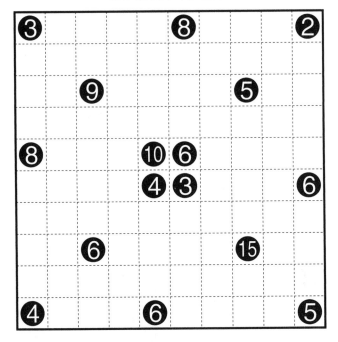

263 EASY

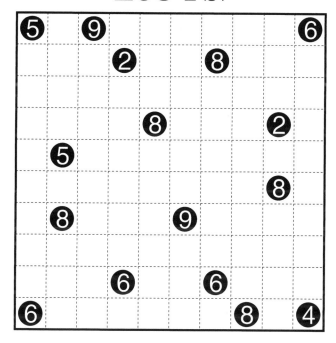

264 EASY

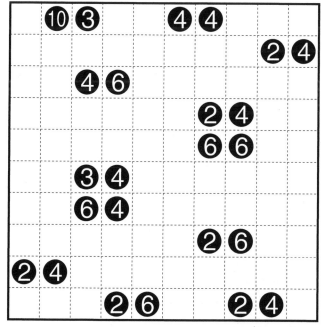

265 EASY

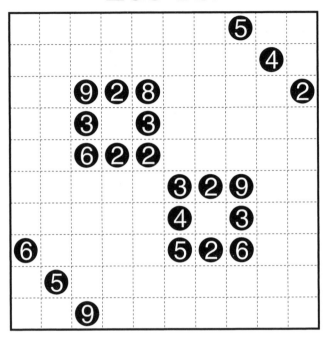

266 EASY

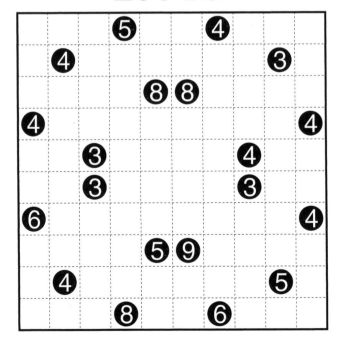

267 EASY

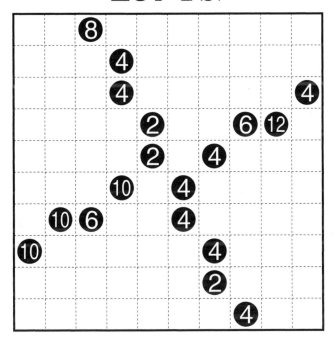

268 EASY

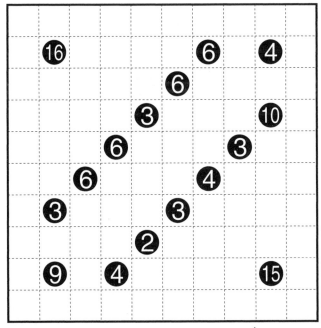

269 EASY

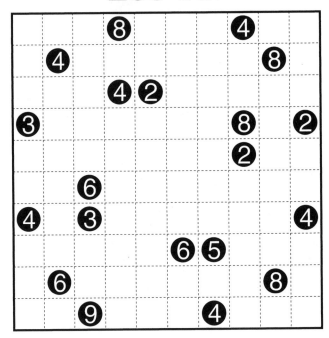

270 EASY

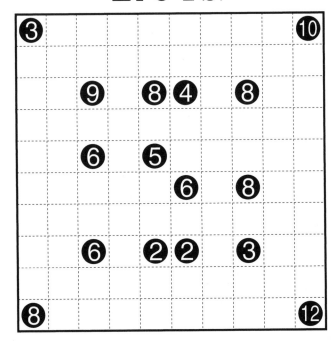

271 MEDIUM

272 MEDIUM

			8				6		3
					4				
			6					2	
	4					4			
4				3			6		
		10							
					4				6
3				4					
			4				8		
		4				4			
					2				4
8				4					
							6		
		6			5				6
			4					10	
	3					6			
				8					
4		5				2			

273 MEDIUM

274 MEDIUM

								5	
	8				2				
		6					6		
				4					6
	6					6			
			9					10	
5					4				3
		5							
				6				6	
	4				3				
							3		
4				2					6
	3					9			
			6					4	
5					4				
		6					3		
				8				4	
	9								

275 MEDIUM

276 MEDIUM

4				5					4				4
						6	6						
		10									4		
						6	2						
3				2					4				4
6				6					4				3
						8	6						
		4									10		
						4	8						
3				4					8				2
					6			4					
	3		4							4		2	
	2		2							4		8	
					4			6					
8				2					4				6
						4	6						
		12									6		
						4	4						
6				6					2				8
6				2					6				3
						3	6						
		8									3		
						6	4						
4				6					4				8

277 MEDIUM

278 HARD

				5					4				
			8							8			
		9									4		
	7											8	
5					2			12					4
				12					3				
			9							4			
						4	2						
	4											6	
		4									12		
6			6			3	3			3			6
					6			2					
					4			2					
6			2			3	6			12			5
		4									6		
	4											4	
						5	6						
			10							4			
				4					2				
4					6			8					6
	8											8	
		4									4		
			4							12			
				6					6				

279 HARD

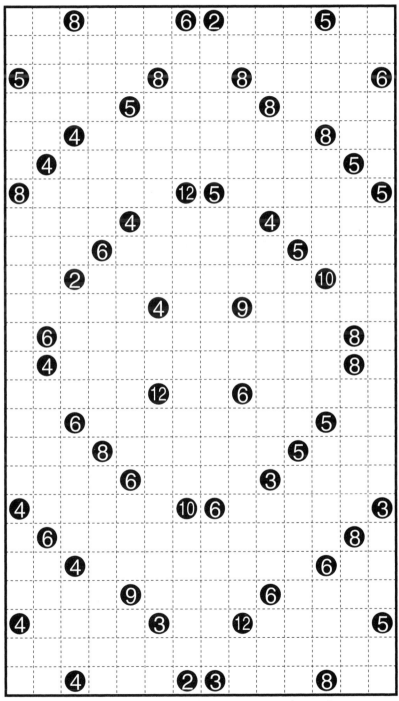

280 HARD

281 HARD

282 HARD

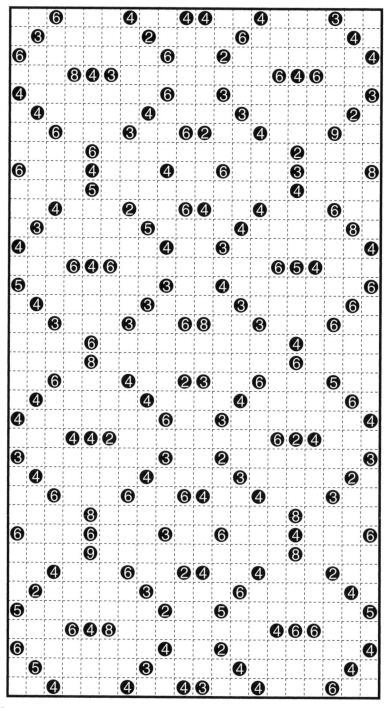

283 HARD

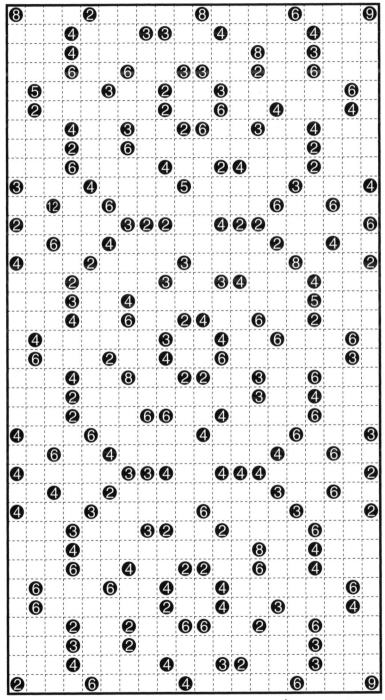

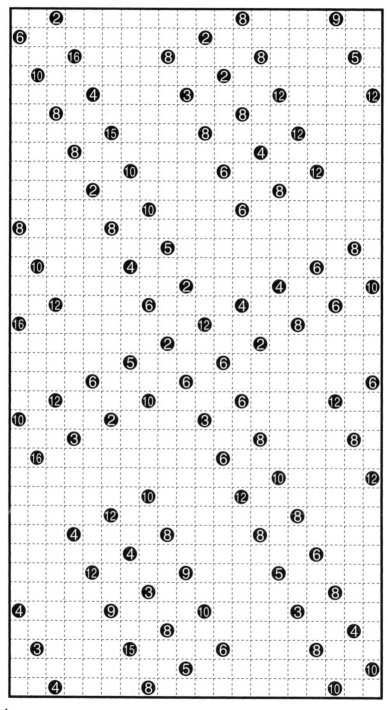

SLITHERLINK

In slitherlink puzzles, you are presented with a grid of dots and numbers. Your goal is to connect the dots with vertical and horizontal lines until you've created a single loop with no crossings or branches, doing so in such a way that each number in the grid is equal to the number of walls surrounding it. That's all there is to it! Of course, although the rules are simple, solving a slitherlink can involve some very complex logic. Let's solve a slitherlink from beginning to end to help you get a feel for it.

Here's a small slitherlink puzzle. A savvy slitherlink solver will be able to fill in a number of lines right away, as shown in the diagram just below the puzzle. (X's represent places where a line cannot go.) How did the solver know where to draw those lines? Well, let's take a closer look at some of the number arrangements in the grid.

Notice that 0 with a 3 next to it in the upper left. Any time you see a 0 that's horizontally or vertically adjacent to a 3, you can fill in lines and X's as shown below left. That's because there can't be a line between the 0 and the 3 (since there are no lines adjacent to the 0), so the other three line segments around the 3 must be filled in, and then must turn as shown. And the line can't branch, so you can draw X's around the corners of the path you've made around the 3.

Now look at the diagonally adjacent 3's in the center of the grid. Any time you have this arrangement of 3's, you can draw L shapes in the two opposite corners, as shown at right. Why? Well, there are four possible ways to place three lines around a square. If you try all four of those ways with either of the diagonally adjacent 3's, you'll see that two of them make it impossible to draw three lines around the other 3

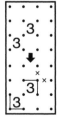

(the top two in the diagram at right). We don't know right away which of the other two possibilities is right, but they each share two of the same lines, so we can fill those two lines in, and do the same with the opposite 3.

What about the adjacent 3's at the top right? Whenever there are two horizontally or vertically adjacent 3's, you can draw three parallel lines and mark the two segments next to the middle line with X's. How do you know to do this? There are only two legal ways to draw lines around two adjacent 3's, and in both, three parallel lines are filled in, and the center line turns at both ends, allowing you to rule out the adjacent line segments.

The other place where lines can be drawn right away is along the bottom edge of the grid, where the 2 is adjacent to the 0. The segment adjacent to the 0 can't be filled in, and the segment along the edge can't be filled in either, because then there would be nowhere for the line to progress without placing a segment next to the 0, which is impossible. So the other two segments around the 2 are filled in, with the line extending one segment further in each direction as shown.

Let's take another look at that slitherlink (shown again, in progress, at right) and see if we can finish it. In the top row, the first 2 has two X's around it, so the other two segments must be filled in. One of those segments extends to the left and connects to an existing line extending up from the 3, and the other one can only proceed in one direction. Extending the line in that direction accounts for both line segments around the other 2 in the top row, so we can fill in X's around it (see right).

We can draw one more X along the top edge next to the two we just wrote in, because there's no place for a line to go from that point. Adding that X leaves only one direction for the line segment along the top edge to go, which means we can draw in the two missing lines

246

for those adjacent 3's. Then we can fill in the two available lines around the 2 just below that and to the right, just like we did in the upper left, and we can connect the two lines heading toward the upper right corner.

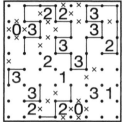

There's now a sequence of spots where filling in one part of the line forces another line to be filled in, or forces the line to move in a particular direction. Look again at the second 2 in the top row. The line around it can only go down, which forces two things: the path it connects to must continue around the 3 to the right, and the segment to its right can now only turn down, connecting to the line around the 3 below it. This forces the path around that 3 to continue up, connecting to the other path (see left).

You can probably see what happens next. The two remaining segments around the 2 in the fourth row can be filled in, after which the line can only extend in one direction from each endpoint. One of those extensions is along the edge of a 1, so you can X out the other three segments around it. That forces the line to move to the left, and now you should be able to fill in the entire bottom left corner (see right).

Almost done! The endpoint next to the 1 can only proceed to the right. Then it has to go down (if it went to the right, the line couldn't continue after drawing three segments around the 3), to the right, and up. That segment going up is the one segment that goes next to the 1, so the line can't turn right, but has to keep going up, and then goes up one more segment to close the loop. Finished!

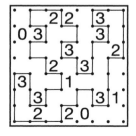

285 EASY

```
      2 0
   3           1 3 3
   0     1
   3     1   3 3 3   2
         3             0
 3               3
 3     2 2 2     0     3
                 1     3
     3 0 3             3
               0 2
```

286 EASY

```
 0 2   3 3   3   3 3
   3     3 0       3 3
   3           3
 1   3   3   3       2
 3       1   3   2   3
         3           0
 3 0       3 3       3
 0 2   3   0 2   3 3
```

```
3   1 1   2
                2 3 1
  3     2 0 3
  0   1
        3       3 0 3
1 3 3       2
              1     1
      0 2 0       3
3 1 3
        0   0 2   3
```

```
  3
  0     3 1 3 1 3 0
  3
  2     3 2
  1   1     2   0
  3   1     3   2
        1 1       1
                  2
2 3 3 3 2 1       0
                  3
```

289 EASY

```
3 3   3     0   0 1
                3
  1 0 3 2 1   0
    3       3       1
  2           2   1   1
  1   1   2           0
  2     2         2
      1   3 0 2 0 2
    2
  2 1   3     1   2 0
```

290 EASY

```
      0 2 3 3
  2   2           2   2
  0   1           1   2
  1     1 3 3 1       1
  1   3           3   2
  0   0           3   3
  2     3 3 3 2       3
  3   3           2   1
  3   1           0   2
      2 1 3 3
```

291 EASY

```
2 1 3 0 3 2 1 1
0               2
3               0
2     1 3       2
1     1 3       0
2               1
2               3
1 3 1 3 0 3 2 1
```

292 EASY

```
2 2         1 1
    3 3         2 3
        1 3
    3 3         1 3
        3 3         3 1
1 1         3 3
    3 3         3 3
        1 3
    3 3         2 2
        2 3         3 2
```

293 EASY

```
  1                    2
0   3 1 1 3 2 3    3
  2                    1
  1       2 3       3
  3     1       2   1
  2     3       2   3
  1         1 2     1
  2                    3
2     3 1 2 3 0 2    3
  1                    3
```

294 EASY

```
  2 2   2       1 2
2 3       0   3   3 2
3               0       2
  3 3 1 2 1 2
      3         3     1 3
1 1   1       2
        1 1 2 3 3 1
3       3                  3
1 2   1     3       2 2
  3 1       0   0 2
```

252

295 EASY

```
3                 3
  1 0 2   0   3
  2         2       1
  1   3       0 1 3
  3     3
                2       0
  2 3 3       2   3
1       0           2
  3   3   2 2 1
      0               0
```

296 EASY

```
  3 2 1 3 2       3
3                     1
    0 3 1       0   2
    3       1   2   2
1       2       0   3
2   3         3     3
3   1 1           2
3   1     3 2 0
2       3             1
  3       1 2 2 0 2
```

297 MEDIUM

	3			1	0			3	
3				3			3		3
		2					1		
0	3				3				2
			1	3			2		1
	2				1		0		
1	3		0					3	
		3			1	3			
1				3				3	3
1	2				2				2
			3	3			0		
	0					3		1	3
		3		1				1	
2		3			3	0			
2				2				2	3
		3					1		
1		0			3				3
	3			2	3			0	

298 MEDIUM

```
  3 2   1 2   1 1

1     3     2     2

1     0     3     3

   1     3 1     3

   1     1 3     1

0     1     1     0

1     1     2     1

  3 3         3 3

0         3 0     1

2         2 2     1

  2 2         1 0

2     3     3     3

2     3     0     3

  0     1 2     1

  2     3 2     3

1     3     1     1

1     2     0     3

  1 0   3 3   2 0
```

```
  3       3 1
0 2     2     3         2 2
1         2 1         2       1
                      0 3
1       2 3
                          2 2       1
    1 0                              2
  1     1         3 1       2 3
      0           1       3
              3         1         1
  1 1       1 3           3       3
  3                       2 3
  1       2 2
                          2 0       3
      1 2
  2       3         2 3             2
  3 3           2       0       3 1
                    2 1       1
```

300 MEDIUM

			1						1
2	0		0		3	1	1		0
			2						2
3						1			
2		3	0	3		0		1	1
3						2			
			3						1
3	2		2		1	1	0		1
			1						0
2						3			
0		3	2	3		3		3	3
1						3			
			3						1
2	3		1		1	1	1		0
			3						1
2						1			
0		1	0	3		0		3	2
1						1			

301 MEDIUM

```
1 1 2 3 1      3 2 2 0 1
3       0      3         3
1       3      3         0
2       2      1         3
    2              2
0     2      0 3      3        0
        2              3
3       3      2         1
0       1      3         3
2       3      2         2
1 3 3 3 1      1 3 3 3 3
2              3 2              0
0              0 1              2
2 0 1 2 1      3 2 0 3 1
1       2      1         0
3       0      3         2
0       3      2         0
    2              2
0     3      0 3      2        0
        3              3
1       1      3         3
3       3      1         3
3       1      2         3
2 3 2 0 1      2 2 1 3 2
```

258

302 MEDIUM

```
3       2       1       0 1 0
3     3   1   2   1   1   2
2     0   2   0   3   2 1 2
1 0       3       3       1

2 3 0     1 2 2 0   3 0 3 1
2   2     2       1   2
2 2 1 3   3       0
          3   3 1       0 3
  3 0     3   3     3       1
0       1 2   3 2     2 2
  1 3     1     1
          2       3     2 1
  3 3     3 0   3   3       3
2       0     2   3     1 1
  3 3     1 3   2
          3       1   3 1 2 2
        2   1     1     2   0
1 3 3 1   2 0 2 0     0 3 1

      2       0       1     1 1
3 2 2   1   1   3   1       3
2     2   2   1   0   3     3
0 2 2     3       3       3
```

304 HARD

			1	1	3							1	
2		2				0		2	0		3		1
3		0		2		3					0		
		2				2					2		3
	1				2			2	0		3		
	1		2		0						1		1
	2				1					2			
1				3			2	0		1		2	1
2		3		0						2			
2				3						3		1	2
	0	1	1				1	0		0			
										2		3	3
1	1		1										
			2		2	0				1	1	1	
1	2		1						3				1
			1						0		0		2
2	2		3		2	0			1				1
			3					0				1	
0		3						2		0		2	
		3		2	0			0				2	
1		1					3				2		
		2					0		2		2		1
2		0		2	0		3				2		2
	3							1	2	1			

305 HARD

```
 3 1       3 2 3 1       2 1
    2    3           3    3
 1    3    1    3 1    1    0    1
    2    2              1    3
 1 3       3 2 2 1       2 2
       1    3           3    1
 2 2       1 2 1 2       3 1
    2    1           2    3
 3    1    1    0 2    2    1    2
    2    3           2    3
 0 2       2 1 3 1       1 2
    2    3           1    3
       2    2           3    2
 2 3       2 1 2 0       2 3
    3    3           2    3
 3    3    2    2 2    1    2    3
    2    2           1    3
 1 3       3 1 1 2       3 2
    2    2           2    3
 1 3       3 1 1 1       1 3
    2    2           0    2
 2    1    2    2 0    2    1    2
    3    3           2    2
 3 1       2 1 1 2       3 3
```

306 HARD

```
  3           1 2           2
  3           3 3           2
    3 1 3           1 0 3
1           2       0           2
1     1 0     2       2 1     0
    3 2     1       0   3 2
          1 3                 3
2       2 0           3 0       1
0     2 3     2       1   3 2     2
      1         3 3         2
          2               3
3 2       3     3 1     1       1 3
3 0         1     2 3     0     3 1
          3                 1
        1         0 2           3
0     1 3     3       2     2 1     3
2         2 1             0 2       1
3               2 3
        0 2     2       2     3 2
1       2 3     3       2     1 3     2
3               3         2           2
    3 1 2               3 0 3
      1             0 1           1
      3             2 3             0
```

2 1 3 　 2 0 　 0 1 1
　 　 3 　 　 0
　 1 　 1 　 3 　 3
　 　 　 1 3
2 1 3 2 　 　 2 1 3 1
　 　 2 　 0
3 　 0 　 3 　 2 　 1 　 3

0 2 0 3 　 1 1 　 2 3 0 3

1
3 　 0 2 1 2 　 3 　 1 　 2
1 　 　 　 2 0 2 1 　 2
0 　 3 　 3 　 　 0

3 3 1 3 　 1 1 　 3 0 2 0

3 　 0 　 3 　 3 　 2 　 1
　 　 1 　 0
2 2 0 3 　 　 1 0 2 3
　 2 0
　 1 　 0 　 2 　 3
　 1 　 3
0 2 2 　 2 0 　 3 2 0

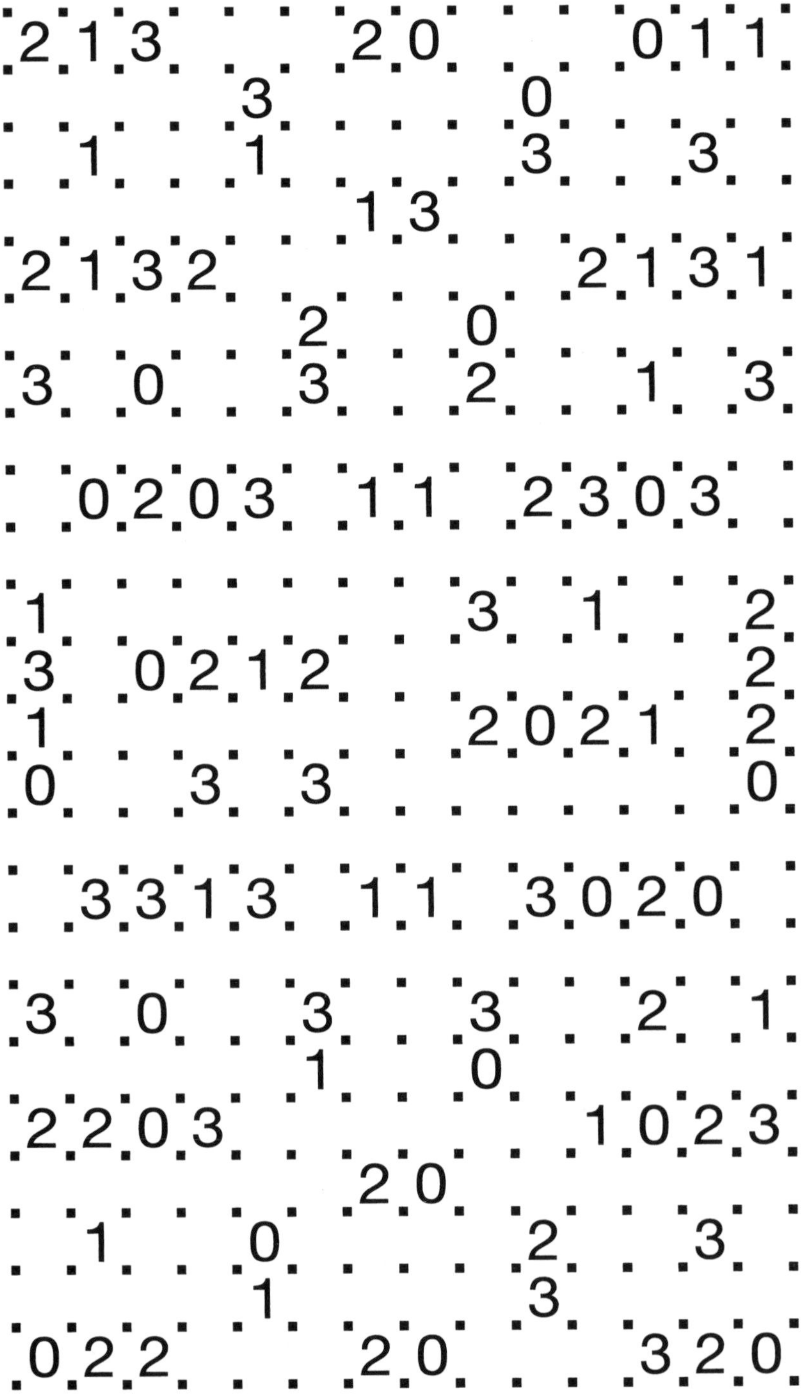

```
  3  3           0  2 1
     2     2        1
     0 3   2 0       3 0 1
 1         1      1          1
 2   1         2     1
     0 2 0         1 0   1 1
                 2       1    2
     2    1 1   2            3
 2   3         1   3 3     1
   1       2       1
       1 1   2 0       0 2 3
           0     1         2
     0         3     1
     2 2 1       1 0   2 2
             3       1     3
 3     0 1   0         3     1
   0         2   1 3   2
 1       0       1
     3 1   3 2       2 1 0
       2       2         1   0
 3         2       2         2
 1 2 2       3 3   1 3
           3       2     0
     2 3   1         1   3
```

309 HARD

2			1			3	1			2			3
	2			3		2	3		3			3	
	0			3					3			1	
		1			2			2			0		
1													0
	3	0			3			2			2	3	
			3			0	2			0			
3						3	3						3
	2		2							2		3	
	1			3	3			0	1			3	
		2				3	3				1		
0				3					3				3
2				3					1				3
		3				2	3				3		
	0			3	0			0	2			3	
	2		2							1		1	
1						3	1						1
			0			2	2			2			
	3	2			3			1			3	3	
2													2
		3			3			2			3		
	1			3					3			1	
	3			1		3	2		3			2	
2			1			3	1			0			2

310 HARD

YAJILIN

A yajilin puzzle is a bit like a maze where you must find the walls yourself. The arrows in the grid, which each share a square with a number, indicate the number of black cells in the direction they're pointing. Multiple arrows may point to the same black square, and there may be black squares that have no arrows pointing to them. No two black cells are horizontally or vertically adjacent, and when the correct cells have been shaded in, a path can be drawn through every remaining empty cell (not through the black cells or arrows), so that the path forms a closed loop that never crosses itself. Working back and forth, by shading cells and extending the path, is the key to solving.

Let's take a look at an easy yajilin puzzle so you can see how it works. This puzzle gives us six clues to start with. Let's start with the zero; it indicates that there are no black squares to the right of the arrow. So we know all three squares to the right of the zero are part of the path, though we don't know how the path will go through them, so we'll just mark all three squares with a dot for now. How about the four 1 clues? The one closest to the bottom doesn't give us much help at the moment—we know that one of the five squares to its left is black, but there's no way to tell which right now. The other three 1s, however, each point to a single square only, so we can shade in those three squares (and place dots in the orthogonally adjacent empty squares, since black squares are never horizontally or vertically adjacent). The last clue left is the 2, which points downward at three squares. Two of those three squares are shaded, but which? Since two black squares can't be adjacent, the top and bottom squares must be shaded in, and the middle square left unshaded. Let's place dots around those last two black squares and take a look at what we've got.

Okay, we've made a lot of progress on placing black squares; let's see what we can do with the path now. Take a look at the empty square between the two black squares we just shaded in (below the 2). We know it's part of the path, and two of the squares around it are already blocked off, so the path must extend to the left and right. You'll find that you'll use a lot of this technique—if a square is part of the path and has only two possible adjacent squares for the path to extend to, it's safe to connect those squares. Corners are a good place to spot opportunities like that. For instance, the black square in the center square of the bottom row has formed two corners (and we know they're part of the path). We can extend the path from each of those squares in the two available directions. This connects each of those squares with the path section that we just drew—which allows us to draw two more lines. The two squares adjacent to the upper of the two black squares below the 2 used to have three available squares adjacent to them, but connecting those paths closes off one of the squares for each, so we can draw a portion of the path through them, giving us a grid that looks like this.

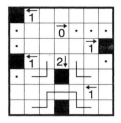

Now that we know the trick with corners, let's see where else we can apply it. All three dotted squares on the left edge of the grid are in corners, as are the two on the right side of the grid, so we can draw paths for them. Of those paths, the one in the upper right extends into the top right corner of the grid, so we can continue that path into the only available square. And are there any places where the path can only extend in one direction? Yes, two: The path segment between the 1 and 2 in the middle row can only go straight up, and in the bottom row, below the 1, the path there can only go to the right, turning up at the corner, and connecting to one of the path segments we just drew. That's a lot of new information, so let's see what we've got now.

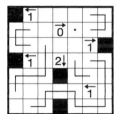

In the lower left, there are two possible ways to link up those two unconnected path segments. How can we tell which is correct? Well, let's not forget about that arrow clue we haven't used yet. Of the five squares that the last 1 arrow points to, we now know that four of them are part of the path—therefore, the one that's left over must be a black square, and the path extends through the other nearby empty square. Let's move from there to the top right. The line segment at the top of the grid could extend in two directions: to the left, or down. But if it went down, it would form a closed loop that didn't connect to the rest of the path, which is impossible; the path must form a single loop. Therefore, it must extend to the left (as does the path segment below it). We can do the same thing to the short path segment in the upper left area of the grid, extending both ends to the right, and incidentally connecting the lower part of that segment to the lower left part of

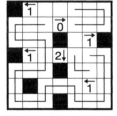

the path. Now look at the square between the zero and 2 in the center column of the grid. With that connection we've just made, three of the four squares around it are blocked off—therefore it's impossible for that square to be part of the path! (Remember, black squares don't necessarily have arrows pointing to them.) Let's shade it in and see what the grid looks like.

Almost done now! The path along the top edge of the grid still can't go down or it will connect with itself, so it must go left and then turn down at the corner

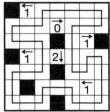

to connect with the next path segment. The other end of the upper right path must go straight down (past the black square we just shaded in), connecting to the path below. That leaves only two loose ends in adjacent squares, so we connect them, and the puzzle is solved!

311 EASY

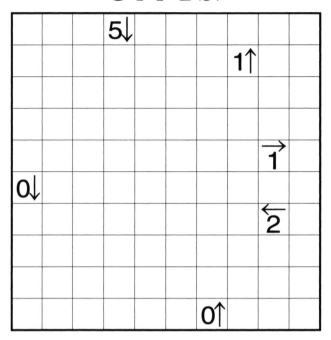

312 EASY

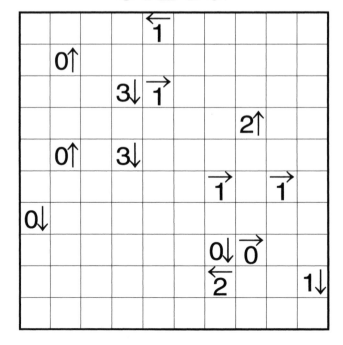

313 EASY

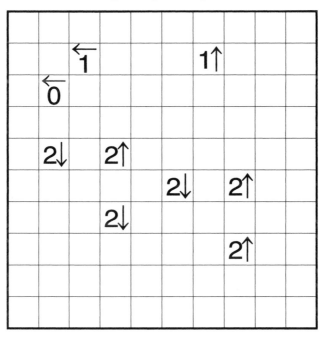

314 EASY

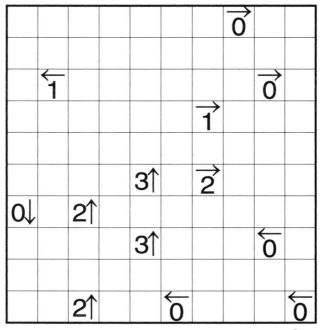

315 EASY

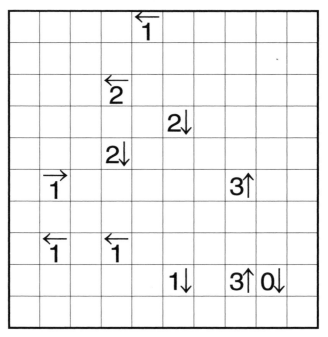

316 EASY

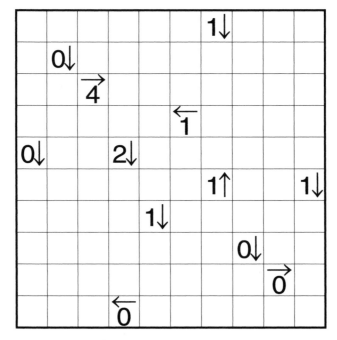

317 EASY

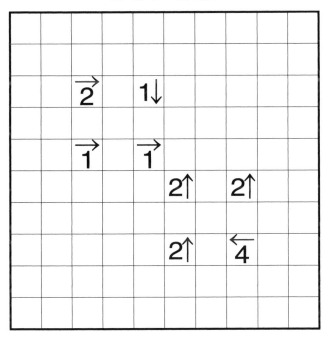

318 EASY

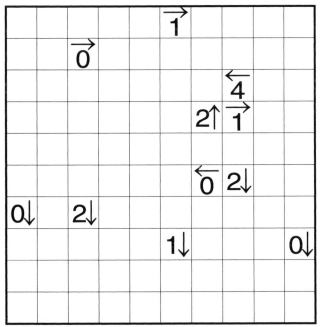

319 EASY

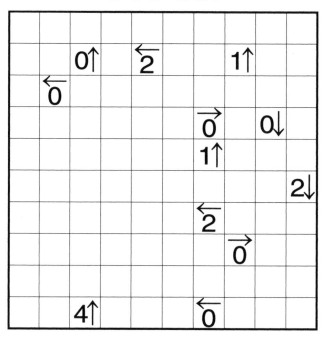

320 EASY

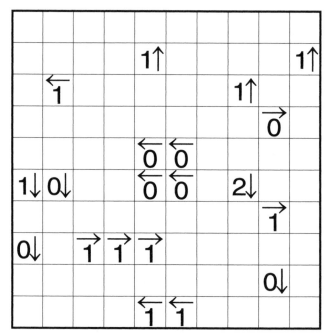

321 EASY

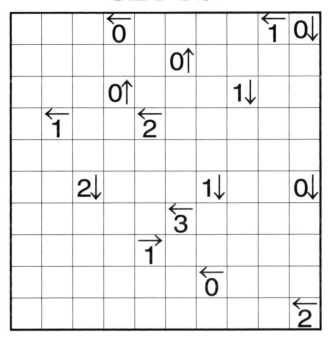

322 EASY

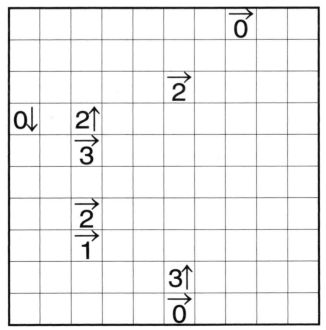

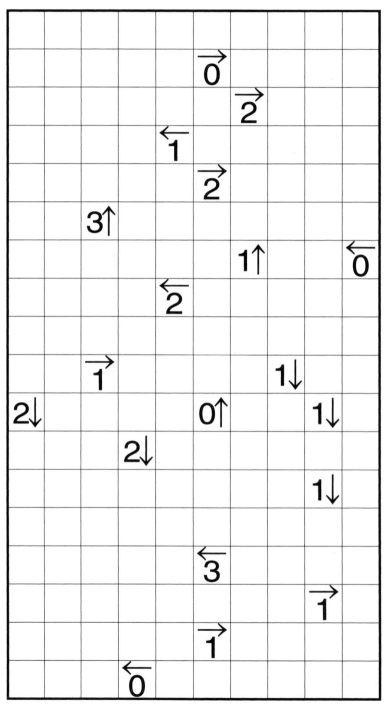

324 MEDIUM

325 MEDIUM

326 MEDIUM

		2↓					
				1↑			
		2↓				1↓	
				2↑			
		2↓				1↓	
0↑				3↑			
		2↓				1↓	
1↑				4↑			
		2↓				1↓	
				4↑			
						1↓	
1↑		1↑	1↑	1↑			
						0↓	
				1↑			
1↑		1↑	1↑			0↓	
				1↑			
			1↑				
1↑		2↑					4↑

327 MEDIUM

0←   0←   1←

0↑

0↑   1↑

2↑   0↑

1↑   1↑   1↑   1←   3↑

2↑   0← 2→ 2→   1→

3←

0←   1→   0→   0↑

2↓ 2→   2→   1→

1←

3→ 2→ 2→ 2→ 1→ 1→   1→

0←

1↓   2→   5↓

0↓   0←   1←

1←   1↓   4↓

1↓   2← 2↓

3↓   1→

1↓   0↓

1←

0↓   3←   3←

2←

280

328 MEDIUM

329 MEDIUM

330 HARD

A Yajilin puzzle grid with directional clues placed in various cells:

					←2					
				←1		1↑				
		←0						0↑		
	1↑				1↑				→1	
			←3			←4				
	←0		←0				→0	←1		
←1										2↓
		←1		→1	→1	→1	→1	2↑	→1	
		←0								
		←1		2↑			→1			
		←0			→0		2↓			2↓
2↑		←0		1↓			→0			
		←1			←1		→0			
							2↓			
		←1	3↓	←1	1↓	3↓	←1	2↓		
3↑									←3	
	2↓		→2				3↑		→0	
			←2			0↓				
	←0				→2			→0		
	1↓							→2		
			←0		1↓					
			←2							

331 HARD

332 HARD

333 HARD

										0→			
		0←		0←									
	0↑				0↑							1↑	
								1↑			0→		
	0←				0←		0←	1→	1↑				
		0←		0→						0→			
			1↑			2↑	1↑		1↑	1→			
		1↑											1←
	1↑												1↑
						2↑	1↑			1↑			
				2←					2↑				
			3↑				2→						1↑
		0→											
						2→				1↑			
					2↓						1↓		
	0→		1↓										
						0↓			1→		1→		
			1↓					1↓				1←	
1↓						2↑							
						2←		1→				1→	
			0↓			1→			1→		1←		
				1→		1←							

334 HARD

335 HARD

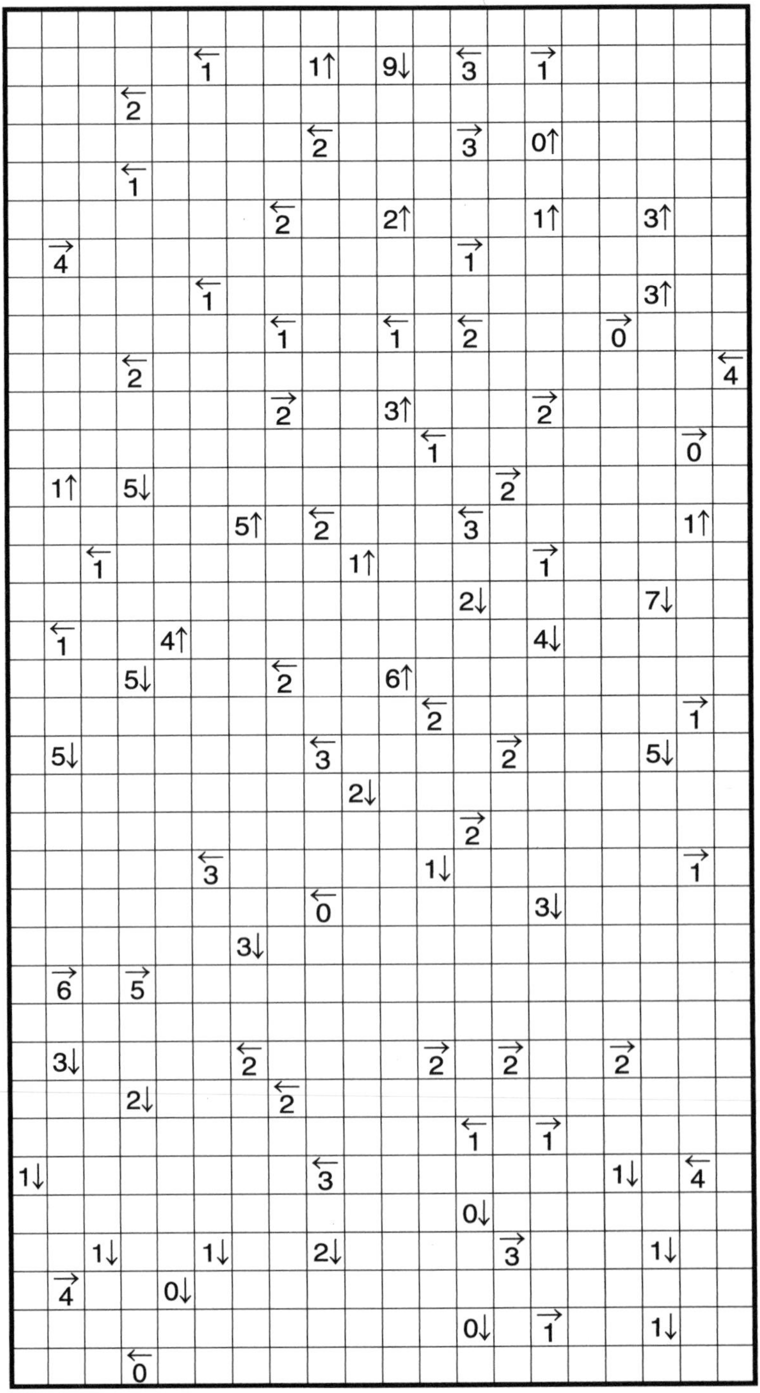

336 HARD

SUDOKU

To solve sudoku puzzles, all you need to know is this one simple rule: **Fill in the boxes so that the nine rows, the nine columns, and the nine 3×3 sections all contain every digit from 1 to 9.**

And that's all there is to it! Using this simple rule, let's see how far we get on this sample puzzle at right. (The letters at the top and left edges of the puzzle are for reference only; you won't see them in the regular puzzles.)

	A	B	C	D	E	F	G	H	I
J									
K				2			1	8	4
L	9		5		7		2		6
M	1		4	3	9	2		7	
N				7		6			
O		7		1	4	8	9		2
P	3		2		6		8		5
Q	8	4	9		3				
R									

The first number that can be filled in is an obvious one: box EN is the only blank box in the center 3×3 section, and all the digits 1 through 9 are represented except for 5. EN must be 5.

The next box is a little trickier to discover. Consider the upper left 3×3 section of the puzzle. Where can a 4 go? It can't go in AK, BK, or CK because row K already has a 4 at IK. It can't go in BJ or BL because column B already has a 4 at BQ. It can't go in CJ because column C already has a 4 at CM. So it must go in AJ.

Another box in that same section that can now be filled is BJ. A 2 can't go in AK, BK, or CK due to the 2 at EK. The 2 at GL rules out a 2 at BL. And the 2 at CP means that a 2 can't go in CJ. So BJ must contain the 2. It is worth noting that this 2 couldn't have been placed without the 4 at AJ in place. Many of the puzzles rely on this type of steppingstone behavior.

	A	B	C	D	E	F	G	H	I
J	4	2							
K				2			1	8	4
L	9		5		7		2		6
M	1		4	3	9	2		7	
N				7	5	6			
O		7		1	4	8	9		2
P	3		2		6		8		5
Q	8	4	9		3				
R									

Let's examine column A. There are four blank boxes in column A; in which blank box must the 2 be placed? It can't be AK because of the 2 in EK (and the 2 in BJ). It can't be AO because of the 2 in IO. It can't be AR because of the 2 in CP. Thus, it must be AN that has the 2. By the 9's in AL, EM, and CQ, box BN must be 9. Do you see how?

We can now determine the value for box IM. Looking at row M and then column I, we find all the digits 1 through 9 are represented but 8. IM must be 8. This brief example of some of the techniques leaves us with the grid at left.

	A	B	C	D	E	F	G	H	I
J	4	2							
K				2			1	8	4
L	9		5		7		2		6
M	1		4	3	9	2		7	8
N	2	9		7	5	6			
O		7		1	4	8	9		2
P	3		2		6		8		5
Q	8	4	9		3				
R									

You should now be able to use what you learned to fill in CN followed by BL, then HL followed by DL and FL.

As you keep going through this puzzle, you'll find it gets easier as you fill in more. And as you keep working through the puzzles in this book, you'll find it gets easier and more fun each time. The final answer is shown here.

	A	B	C	D	E	F	G	H	I
J	4	2	1	6	8	3	5	9	7
K	7	3	6	5	2	9	1	8	4
L	9	8	5	4	7	1	2	3	6
M	1	5	4	3	9	2	6	7	8
N	2	9	8	7	5	6	4	1	3
O	6	7	3	1	4	8	9	5	2
P	3	1	2	9	6	7	8	4	5
Q	8	4	9	2	3	5	7	6	1
R	5	6	7	8	1	4	3	2	9

		8					4	7
	1			3	8	2		
	5		1					3
2				7		8	9	
				1				
	9	6	3					2
8					2		6	
		9	6	5				1
3	6					4		

338 EASY

				1				
		4	5			7	6	
	1		9		7		8	
		2	4			3	1	
				3				
	7	1			2	5		
	6		1		5		7	
	5	8			6	2		
				2				

339 EASY

	9			6			8	
1	5			9			4	7
			2		5			
		7	1		9	3		
6	3						1	4
		5	6		8	7		
			3		1			
9	7			5			6	8
	8			7			2	

340 EASY

		4	5	2				
1	5						4	6
				6	7	5		
	3	1	8					
6								3
					5	2	1	
	3	1	8					
5	2						6	7
				5	2	4		

292

336 HARD

SUDOKU

To solve sudoku puzzles, all you need to know is this one simple rule: **Fill in the boxes so that the nine rows, the nine columns, and the nine 3×3 sections all contain every digit from 1 to 9.**

And that's all there is to it! Using this simple rule, let's see how far we get on this sample puzzle at right. (The letters at the top and left edges of the puzzle are for reference only; you won't see them in the regular puzzles.)

	A	B	C	D	E	F	G	H	I
J									
K					2		1	8	4
L	9		5		7		2		6
M	1		4	3	9	2		7	
N				7		6			
O		7		1	4	8	9		2
P	3		2		6		8		5
Q	8	4	9		3				
R									

The first number that can be filled in is an obvious one: box EN is the only blank box in the center 3×3 section, and all the digits 1 through 9 are represented except for 5. EN must be 5.

The next box is a little trickier to discover. Consider the upper left 3×3 section of the puzzle. Where can a 4 go? It can't go in AK, BK, or CK because row K already has a 4 at IK. It can't go in BJ or BL because column B already has a 4 at BQ. It can't go in CJ because column C already has a 4 at CM. So it must go in AJ.

Another box in that same section that can now be filled is BJ. A 2 can't go in AK, BK, or CK due to the 2 at EK. The 2 at GL rules out a 2 at BL. And the 2 at CP means that a 2 can't go in CJ. So BJ must contain the 2. It is worth noting that this 2 couldn't have been placed without the 4 at AJ in place. Many of the puzzles rely on this type of steppingstone behavior.

	A	B	C	D	E	F	G	H	I
J	4	2							
K					2		1	8	4
L	9		5		7		2		6
M	1		4	3	9	2		7	
N				7	5	6			
O		7		1	4	8	9		2
P	3		2		6		8		5
Q	8	4	9		3				
R									

Let's examine column A. There are four blank boxes in column A; in which blank box must the 2 be placed? It can't be AK because of the 2 in EK (and the 2 in BJ). It can't be AO because of the 2 in IO. It can't be AR because of the 2 in CP. Thus, it must be AN that has the 2. By the 9's in AL, EM, and CQ, box BN must be 9. Do you see how?

We can now determine the value for box IM. Looking at row M and then column I, we find all the digits 1 through 9 are represented but 8. IM must be 8. This brief example of some of the techniques leaves us with the grid at left.

	A	B	C	D	E	F	G	H	I
J	4	2							
K					2		1	8	4
L	9		5		7		2		6
M	1		4	3	9	2		7	8
N	2	9		7	5	6			
O		7		1	4	8	9		2
P	3		2		6		8		5
Q	8	4	9		3				
R									

You should now be able to use what you learned to fill in CN followed by BL, then HL followed by DL and FL.

As you keep going through this puzzle, you'll find it gets easier as you fill in more. And as you keep working through the puzzles in this book, you'll find it gets easier and more fun each time. The final answer is shown here.

	A	B	C	D	E	F	G	H	I
J	4	2	1	6	8	3	5	9	7
K	7	3	6	5	2	9	1	8	4
L	9	8	5	4	7	1	2	3	6
M	1	5	4	3	9	2	6	7	8
N	2	9	8	7	5	6	4	1	3
O	6	7	3	1	4	8	9	5	2
P	3	1	2	9	6	7	8	4	5
Q	8	4	9	2	3	5	7	6	1
R	5	6	7	8	1	4	3	2	9

337 EASY

		8					4	7
1				3	8	2		
5			1					3
2					7	8	9	
				1				
	9	6	3					2
8					2		6	
		9	6	5			1	
3	6					4		

338 EASY

				1				
		4	5			7	6	
	1		9		7		8	
		2	4			3	1	
				3				
	7	1			2	5		
	6		1		5		7	
	5	8			6	2		
				2				

339 EASY

	9			6			8	
1	5			9			4	7
			2		5			
		7	1		9	3		
6	3						1	4
		5	6		8	7		
			3		1			
9	7			5			6	8
	8			7			2	

340 EASY

		4	5	2				
1	5						4	6
			6	7	5			
	3	1	8					
6								3
				5	2	1		
	3	1	8					
5	2						6	7
			5	2	4			

341 EASY

		7				4		
	8		1		7		3	
5				2				1
	9		4		3		6	
		2				5		
	6		5		2		4	
1				6				2
	2		3		4		5	
		8				7		

342 EASY

	1				8	7		
		3	2				9	
7				3			8	
	9	8			3			4
			8		4			
2			9			5	6	
	2			4				3
	7				9	1		
		6	5				4	

	6			5				
9						8	4	
		4	3			2	1	
		3	4					
8	5						6	7
					7	9		
	1	5			8	3		
	7	2						9
				6			2	

344 EASY

	9	8	7					
1				2	3	4		
2							6	
3							2	
	6			7			8	
	7							4
	8							9
		4	5	6				7
					8	5	1	

345 MEDIUM

				8				
3				9		1	6	
	4				5			2
		1			2			
8		6				7		9
			3			4		
9			6				3	
	2	8		4				5
				1				

346 MEDIUM

	2	7	6					
				1				5
			7		8			9
		1				4		7
	3			2			6	
4		5				1		
1			4		5			
9				8				
						1	3	2

347 MEDIUM

3					7	5		1
					2	9		
4	8							
1	2		3		4			
			5		6		7	8
							4	2
		6	9					
5		7	1					6

348 MEDIUM

		1	6					
	5		7			1	9	
3		2			9	4		
6				4	8	9		
	4						2	
		5	3	7				1
		9	2			8		3
	7	8			1		6	
					5	7		

349 MEDIUM

					8			
		4			5	3		
7						6		
2	9							
8			7		2			9
							6	5
		5						8
		3	6			4		
			2					

350 MEDIUM

	4	5	1					
				3				8
				2			7	3
	2	9	7					4
8					1	3	6	
1	8			6				
7				5				
					4	6	9	

Sudoku 数独 297

351 MEDIUM

7			2					
			3			6	4	
		8			4		1	
5	9			2		3		
			6		5			
		4		7			5	8
	2		9			7		
	8	1				3		
					2			4

352 MEDIUM

		2	3				5	
	1			4				
9					5		2	
8			7	6			3	
7								4
	6			3	4			5
	5		2					6
				1			7	
	7				9	8		

353 HARD

5				9			3	
7					5	6		
		4						1
			5		4	8	1	
4								3
	8	9	3		2			
6						2		
		7	2					8
	4			8				6

354 HARD

	9	1	7					
							6	
		4			8			2
			1			5		7
1				8				9
2		3			4			
7			2			8		
	5							
						3	4	9

355 HARD

	9							5
		8	6		1			
							2	
	7				9			4
		3				6		
2			5				9	
	1							
			4		3	8		
5							1	

356 HARD

			5		1			
	9		7		4		3	
		3				2		
3	2						7	1
9	1						2	6
		6				8		
	5		4		2		9	
			3		7			

357 HARD

	2	3			7		5	
1					6			4
			4	5				3
6								
		8	9		4	3		
								1
7				4	3			
8			5					6
	9		6			8	7	

358 HARD

		3	8	2				
		6		1	9	5	7	
		8					6	
	5	2				8	3	
	9					4		
7	4	5	8		2			
			3	2	6			

359 HARD

							6	
1	4					5	7	
	2	5			4	8		
		3	6		9			
			8					
			7		1	2		
		8	5			3	4	
	9	4					5	6
	3							

360 HARD

			5	3	2	8		
				1				4
					7			6
							1	8
1								3
2	5							
3		8						
7			6					
	6	9	4	2				

ANSWERS

AKARI

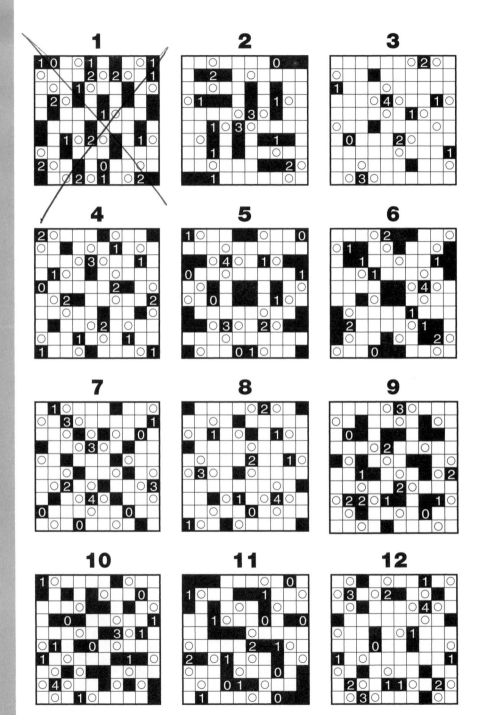

13

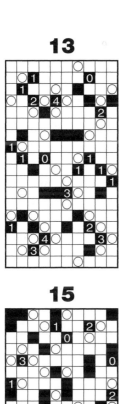

14

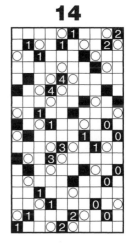

15

16

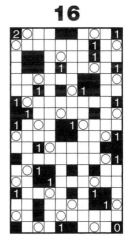

17

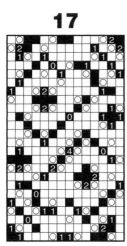

18

19

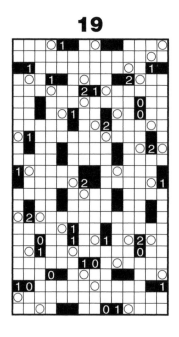

20

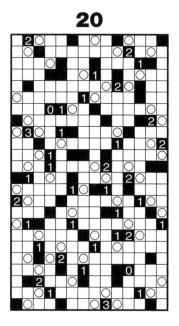

21

22

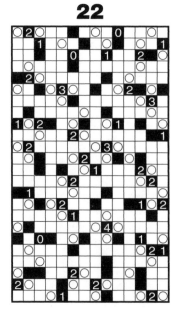

23

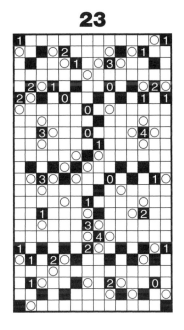

24

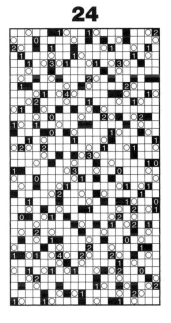

25

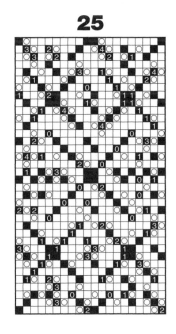

26

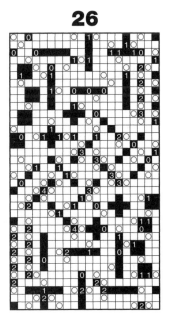

FILLOMINO

27

```
3 2 3 3 1 4 2 2 1 5
3 2 3 1 3 4 3 3 3 5
3 1 2 2 3 4 2 2 5 5
7 2 7 1 3 4 3 3 5 2
7 2 7 2 2 5 3 4 4 2
7 7 7 5 5 5 4 4 1 4
3 4 4 4 5 3 3 3 4 4
3 3 1 4 3 2 1 2 2 4
1 2 2 3 3 2 3 3 1 3
3 3 3 2 2 1 3 1 3 3
```

28

```
3 3 1 3 3 1 3 3 6 6
6 3 2 5 3 5 6 3 6 4
6 6 2 5 5 5 6 2 6 4
4 6 6 2 2 6 6 2 6 4
4 3 6 3 3 6 3 3 6 4
4 3 2 2 3 6 3 2 2 1
4 3 1 6 6 4 4 4 3 2
2 4 2 2 6 3 4 3 3 2
2 4 4 4 6 3 3 4 4 4
3 3 3 6 6 2 2 4 2 2
```

29

```
2 4 4 4 3 3 5 5 5 5
2 5 5 4 3 5 2 4 4 5
5 5 3 3 5 5 2 4 3 3
5 4 1 3 5 5 1 4 3 2
4 4 4 2 3 3 3 5 5 2
3 3 3 2 1 7 7 3 5 5
2 4 4 4 7 7 3 3 5 3
2 4 6 7 7 5 5 5 3 3
6 1 6 7 5 5 6 6 6 6
6 6 6 3 3 3 3 6 2 2 6
```

30

```
4 4 4 3 3 5 3 1 4 1
4 3 3 4 3 5 3 6 4 3
1 3 2 4 4 5 3 6 4 3
4 1 2 4 5 5 2 6 4 3
4 2 1 2 3 3 2 6 3 1
4 2 5 2 1 3 6 6 3 3
4 3 5 5 5 2 3 3 1 6
3 3 4 2 4 1 2 3 3 6
4 4 4 2 4 3 1 2 2 6
3 3 3 4 4 3 3 6 6 6
```

31

```
5 5 6 6 6 2 2 4 6 6
5 3 3 3 6 6 6 4 4 6
5 5 5 6 1 3 3 3 4 6
1 3 3 6 6 6 6 1 2 6
5 5 3 2 2 1 3 3 2 6
1 5 5 5 6 6 1 3 4 1
5 1 2 2 6 3 3 4 4 1
5 5 5 5 6 5 3 5 2 4
2 2 1 6 6 5 5 5 2 4
5 5 5 5 5 1 2 2 4 4
```

32

```
5 5 6 6 6 6 6 5 5 5
5 3 3 6 3 3 3 6 4 5
5 5 3 2 6 6 6 6 4 5
6 6 6 2 1 6 4 2 4 4
5 4 6 6 6 4 4 2 1 2
5 4 4 2 2 4 1 4 4 2
5 4 5 4 4 3 4 3 3 3
5 1 5 5 4 3 3 1 3 1
5 4 1 5 4 2 4 4 4 3
4 4 4 5 1 2 4 1 3 3
```

33

```
1 2 5 5 5 1 5 5 2 4
6 2 5 6 5 2 5 1 2 4
6 6 6 3 2 5 5 4 4 4
2 2 5 2 3 5 1 2 2 3
5 5 5 2 3 5 5 5 5 3
5 2 2 4 4 3 3 4 4 3
2 1 4 1 4 3 4 4 2 2
2 4 4 3 4 6 6 6 6 6
3 4 3 3 1 3 3 5 6 5
3 3 4 4 4 4 3 5 5 5
```

34

```
2 3 4 4 4 2 4 2 1 2
2 3 3 1 4 2 4 2 6 2
3 4 1 2 2 1 4 4 6 6
3 4 2 5 5 4 1 2 6 3
3 4 2 5 5 4 4 2 6 3
2 4 3 5 3 3 4 1 6 3
2 3 3 1 3 1 2 2 3 2
4 4 4 5 1 3 3 5 3 2
4 3 5 5 5 3 1 5 3 1
3 3 5 2 2 5 5 5 2 2
```

35

```
1 5 8 2 1 2 2 9 9 9
2 5 8 2 5 1 5 5 5 9
2 5 8 5 5 4 5 2 9 9
5 5 8 5 5 4 5 2 9 2
4 4 8 8 8 4 4 3 9 2
4 5 4 4 8 1 3 3 9 1
4 5 4 4 5 4 4 4 3 3
5 5 1 5 5 5 2 4 3 6
5 2 2 5 4 4 2 6 1 6
4 4 4 4 1 4 4 6 6 6
```

36

```
3 1 2 2 1 2 7 7 6 6
3 2 3 3 2 7 6 6 6
3 2 4 4 7 7 7 3 1 6
1 4 1 4 4 7 3 3 2 2
3 4 4 5 5 5 2 2 3 3
3 3 4 1 4 5 5 4 4 3
5 5 5 5 4 1 4 4 7 7
4 2 1 5 4 4 1 2 2 7
4 2 6 6 6 6 6 6 7 7
4 4 1 2 2 3 3 3 7 7
```

37

```
4 2 3 3 3 4 4 4 5 5
4 2 4 4 4 1 5 4 2 5
4 1 2 4 2 2 5 5 2 5
4 5 2 5 6 6 2 5 6 5
2 5 5 5 2 6 2 5 6 6
2 1 2 1 2 6 6 6 1 6
5 5 2 5 5 5 2 1 6 6
4 5 5 1 5 5 5 2 1 3
4 5 2 5 2 2 1 2 3 3
4 4 2 5 5 5 5 1 2 2
```

38

```
6 6 6 6 5 2 2 4 4 4
6 4 4 4 5 5 5 4 2 2
6 2 4 1 6 5 2 2 3 3
3 2 6 6 6 6 3 3 4 3
3 3 1 3 1 6 4 3 4 4
2 2 3 3 6 3 4 4 3 4
5 5 5 5 6 3 2 4 3 3
3 5 3 3 6 3 2 1 4 4
3 3 4 3 6 6 1 2 2 4
4 4 4 2 2 6 3 3 3 4
```

308

39

```
4 4 4 2 3 2 3 3 3
3 2 1 6 2 3 2 5 4 4
3 2 6 6 6 3 5 5 1 4
3 5 5 5 6 6 5 6 6 4
5 5 4 4 4 2 5 4 6 6
2 2 8 8 4 2 4 4 5 6
3 8 8 3 3 3 4 2 5 6
3 8 3 1 5 5 5 2 5 5
3 8 3 3 5 1 5 1 6 5
8 8 4 4 1 5 2 2 6 2
2 5 5 4 4 5 4 1 6 2
2 5 5 7 5 5 4 6 6 6
1 2 5 7 5 4 4 2 4 4
3 2 1 7 3 3 1 2 5 4
3 3 7 7 1 3 2 5 5 4
4 1 7 6 6 6 2 5 1 3
4 4 7 6 6 3 3 5 4 3
4 3 3 3 6 3 4 4 4 3
```

40

```
4 4 2 4 4 4 4 3 6 6
4 4 2 3 3 2 1 3 3 6
5 2 4 4 3 2 3 2 5 6
5 2 1 4 4 3 3 2 5 6
5 3 5 5 5 1 5 5 5 6
5 3 3 4 5 4 4 4 4 3
5 4 4 4 5 3 3 2 3 3
3 3 3 2 2 1 3 2 6 6
7 7 3 3 2 2 6 6 6 3
2 2 7 7 3 4 3 6 6 3
7 7 2 7 7 4 3 4 1 3
7 7 2 3 3 4 3 4 4 4
4 7 7 7 3 4 2 2 6 5
4 4 4 1 7 3 6 6 6 5
5 1 2 2 7 3 6 5 5 5
5 2 4 4 7 3 6 1 4 4
5 2 4 2 7 4 4 4 2 4
5 5 4 2 7 7 7 4 2 4
```

41

```
3 4 3 3 6 6 6 6 6 5
3 4 3 1 3 3 4 4 6 5
3 4 2 2 1 3 4 4 5 5
7 4 3 3 3 1 5 2 3 5
7 7 7 7 2 2 5 2 3 3
1 2 4 7 3 1 5 5 5 1
3 2 4 7 3 3 4 3 3 2
3 4 4 1 4 4 4 5 3 2
3 5 5 4 5 5 5 5 6 6
5 5 5 4 4 6 6 2 1 6
3 1 2 2 4 3 6 2 6 6
3 4 3 3 1 3 6 1 6 2
3 4 2 3 4 3 6 2 3 2
4 4 2 4 4 4 6 2 3 3
2 2 3 1 2 2 3 3 4 4
5 5 3 3 1 4 3 1 4 4
5 4 4 4 3 4 4 4 5 2
5 5 4 3 3 5 5 5 5 2
```

42

```
2 2 3 2 2 5 5 5 4 4
4 4 3 3 5 5 4 3 3 4
4 4 5 5 3 3 4 4 3 4
5 5 5 6 2 3 5 4 2 2
2 2 6 6 2 5 5 5 4 4
5 6 6 2 4 5 1 4 4 8
5 6 5 2 4 4 5 5 3 8
5 1 5 5 2 4 5 3 3 8
5 5 1 5 2 5 5 4 8 8
2 3 2 5 3 3 4 4 8 2
2 3 2 1 5 3 4 8 8 2
1 3 4 5 5 7 7 3 4 4
3 4 4 4 5 7 3 3 4 4
3 3 2 2 5 7 7 7 3 3
2 2 4 4 4 7 4 4 3 2
5 5 4 3 3 4 1 4 4 2
5 2 2 3 4 4 4 2 2 3
5 5 6 6 6 6 6 6 3 3
```

43

```
4 5 3 3 2 3 6 3 2 3
4 5 5 3 2 3 6 3 2 3
4 4 5 2 4 3 6 3 1 3
2 2 5 2 4 4 6 6 6 4
4 5 4 4 1 1 5 2 4 4
4 5 5 4 4 5 5 2 1 4
4 4 5 1 5 5 4 4 4 5
3 3 5 6 1 6 4 5 5 5
4 3 6 6 6 6 1 5 3 3
4 4 2 4 1 7 7 2 3 5
1 4 2 4 4 4 7 2 1 5
2 2 1 7 7 7 7 6 3 5
6 6 2 4 4 4 6 6 3 5
2 6 2 4 6 6 6 4 3 5
2 6 6 6 3 3 3 4 4 1
1 2 2 1 6 6 6 4 1 4
2 4 4 6 6 1 3 2 4 4
2 4 4 6 1 3 3 2 4 1
```

44

```
6 1 3 3 2 6 5 5 5 7
6 2 2 3 2 6 5 2 7 7
6 1 6 6 6 6 5 2 7 7
6 3 3 7 7 4 7 4 7 1
6 6 3 7 4 7 4 4 4 7
2 2 7 7 4 4 3 3 7 7
4 4 6 5 5 4 3 7 7 1
4 6 6 5 3 3 7 7 8 7
4 6 5 5 3 4 4 8 8 7
1 6 6 1 2 4 8 8 7 7
5 5 5 5 2 4 8 7 7 6
5 1 2 2 5 8 8 7 6 6
4 5 5 5 5 5 3 3 3 1 6
4 4 4 2 2 5 5 5 6 6
5 5 5 4 4 5 4 4 4 1
5 2 2 3 4 5 4 6 6 6
5 1 3 3 4 6 3 2 2 6
1 6 6 6 6 6 3 3 6 6
```

45

```
8 8 8 2 8 1 8 8 2 2
2 8 8 2 8 8 8 2 5 5
2 8 2 4 2 8 8 2 5 5
8 8 2 4 2 4 3 3 2 5
2 2 4 4 3 4 4 3 2 3
8 8 8 3 3 2 4 5 5 3
8 2 8 4 4 2 5 5 5 3
6 2 8 8 4 4 2 2 4 2
6 3 4 8 2 2 4 4 4 2
6 3 4 1 4 4 2 2 3 3
6 3 4 4 1 4 4 3 2 3
6 6 3 3 2 2 3 3 2 4
2 1 3 1 3 3 2 4 4 4
2 3 2 3 1 3 2 1 2 2
3 3 2 3 3 1 3 2 3 3
2 2 3 5 5 3 3 2 1 3
3 1 3 3 5 5 5 3 3 2
3 3 2 2 3 3 3 1 3 2
```

46

```
4 2 2 1 2 2 7 1 6 6
4 3 3 7 7 7 7 6 6 6
4 3 1 3 2 2 7 7 3 6
4 1 4 3 3 6 6 3 3 4
2 2 4 2 2 6 2 2 4 4
5 4 4 3 6 6 3 1 4 2
5 5 5 3 3 6 3 3 1 2
5 4 4 2 2 7 7 7 7 7
2 4 3 2 6 7 7 3 3 1
2 3 3 2 6 7 1 3 2 3
4 4 6 6 6 3 3 1 2 3
1 4 4 6 4 4 3 5 5 3
8 2 2 4 4 5 5 5 1 2
8 7 7 7 4 4 4 3 3 2
8 5 5 7 7 7 4 3 4 4
8 5 1 3 3 3 4 2 2 4
8 5 5 2 5 5 5 5 1 4
8 8 8 2 5 4 4 4 4 1
```

47

```
4 2 2 1 2 5 5 5 2 2
4 4 1 4 2 5 5 4 4 4
4 2 4 4 1 2 2 3 4 1
1 2 1 4 3 3 4 3 1 4
4 4 4 3 2 3 4 3 4 4
4 1 3 3 2 4 4 2 4 1
3 4 4 4 3 3 3 2 3 8
3 2 4 2 2 6 6 3 3 8
3 2 8 8 8 8 6 8 8 8
8 8 8 5 5 6 6 8 3 6
8 2 2 5 1 6 8 8 3 6
4 4 5 5 6 1 6 6 3 6
1 4 3 3 6 6 6 3 6 6
2 4 3 5 5 5 2 3 6 4
2 1 2 2 3 5 2 3 4 4
3 4 4 3 3 5 4 4 3 4
3 4 2 2 1 3 3 4 3 2
3 4 3 3 3 1 3 4 3 2
```

48

```
2 3 3 3 6 6 6 5 5 1
2 1 2 2 6 2 2 5 2 2
3 3 3 7 6 6 5 5 3 3
5 5 7 7 7 3 3 3 1 3
3 5 3 3 7 5 9 9 9 9
3 5 1 3 7 5 9 3 3 9
3 5 3 2 7 5 9 3 9 9
5 3 3 2 5 5 4 4 1 5
5 5 5 5 4 4 2 4 5 5
6 6 3 2 2 4 2 4 3 5
6 3 3 7 7 4 1 3 3 5
6 6 4 5 7 7 7 2 2 1
6 4 4 5 7 8 2 5 5 5
1 4 5 5 7 8 2 5 3 5
3 3 5 1 5 8 8 8 3 3
1 3 4 5 5 5 8 5 5 5
3 4 4 3 3 5 8 8 2 5
3 3 4 3 1 3 3 3 2 5
```

49

```
3 3 3 4 4 4 3 1 3 3
4 4 4 3 3 4 3 3 5 3
4 3 1 3 2 2 5 5 5 5
1 3 3 2 4 4 3 3 2 2
3 4 4 2 4 4 3 2 9 9
3 3 4 4 5 5 5 2 9 9
2 2 5 5 3 3 5 5 9 3
3 3 5 5 3 5 3 3 9 3
8 3 5 1 5 5 5 3 9 3
8 8 1 2 1 5 2 2 9 9
3 8 8 2 4 4 6 6 2 2
3 8 2 1 2 4 2 6 6 6
3 8 2 3 2 4 2 6 5 2
1 8 3 3 5 5 1 4 5 2
3 4 4 4 4 5 5 4 5 5
3 3 2 1 3 5 7 4 5 2
4 4 2 4 3 3 7 4 7 2
4 4 1 4 4 4 7 7 7 7
```

50

```
4 4 1 1 3 6 1 3 3 2 3 1 3 3
4 5 5 2 3 6 6 1 3 2 3 4 3 1
1 2 5 2 3 6 2 3 4 4 3 4 4 4
3 2 5 4 2 6 2 3 3 4 2 5 5 1
3 3 5 4 2 6 1 2 2 4 2 3 5 5
2 1 4 4 1 4 4 3 3 3 5 3 3 5
2 5 5 5 4 4 3 5 5 5 5 4 2 1
3 2 5 8 3 1 3 3 1 3 3 4 2 4
3 2 5 8 3 3 5 1 5 3 4 4 1 4
3 8 8 8 4 5 5 5 6 1 2 4 4 ...
1 6 8 3 3 4 6 6 6 6 3 2 1 2
6 6 8 3 4 4 6 1 4 1 3 3 4 2
6 5 5 4 3 3 3 6 4 4 2 1 4 4
6 6 5 4 4 6 6 6 4 1 2 3 3 4
2 5 5 4 1 3 6 1 6 5 5 5 3 6
2 4 2 2 3 3 6 5 6 5 2 6 6 6
4 4 1 4 4 2 2 5 6 5 2 3 2 6
4 1 3 4 3 3 1 5 6 6 3 3 2 6
2 3 3 4 3 5 2 5 4 6 1 6 6 4
2 1 2 2 5 5 2 5 4 3 3 6 3 4
3 3 3 5 5 3 3 3 4 4 3 6 3 4
2 2 1 2 2 1 2 2 3 3 6 6 3 4
1 3 3 4 4 4 3 1 3 4 4 4 4 6
2 2 3 2 2 4 3 3 1 6 6 6 6 6
```

51

```
5 5 4 4 5 5 7 7 2 7 7 7 7
2 5 5 4 5 5 7 4 4 2 7 5 2 7
2 1 5 4 6 5 7 4 2 4 2 5 5 2
4 4 4 6 6 7 7 4 2 4 2 5 5 2
4 6 6 6 5 1 1 5 5 5 4 4 5 1 2
5 3 3 3 5 5 7 5 4 3 3 3 5 4
5 5 5 5 3 5 7 5 4 5 5 5 5 4
3 3 1 1 3 5 7 7 4 4 6 6 6 4
4 3 4 4 4 4 3 7 7 7 6 2 2 4
4 4 1 1 5 5 6 3 3 4 6 6 4 4 2
7 4 6 6 5 6 6 6 6 4 4 5 4 1 2
7 7 4 6 5 5 4 6 6 4 5 4 6 6
7 4 4 6 6 4 4 3 4 5 5 5 6 5
7 4 3 6 5 5 4 3 4 4 6 6 6 5
7 7 3 3 5 5 5 3 4 5 5 3 3 5
3 3 4 4 3 3 3 2 2 1 5 3 5 5
3 2 2 4 4 5 5 5 1 5 5 4 4 3
6 6 6 6 6 2 2 5 4 4 6 6 4 3
6 7 7 7 7 6 5 1 1 4 6 6 4 3
3 7 5 5 6 7 6 1 4 3 6 6 6 5
3 3 5 2 6 6 6 3 4 3 5 5 5 5
4 5 5 2 4 4 3 3 4 3 6 6 6 4
4 2 2 5 5 4 4 1 4 6 6 4 4 4
4 4 5 5 5 3 3 3 2 2 6 2 2 1
```

52

```
4 4 1 4 4 1 4 4 4 3 3 3 2 1
4 6 4 4 3 3 2 2 4 1 4 4 2 4
4 6 6 6 4 3 4 4 3 4 2 3 3 4
6 6 4 4 4 6 3 4 3 2 2 1 3 4
1 3 6 6 6 6 3 4 3 4 4 4 2 4
6 3 3 2 3 6 3 5 1 3 4 1 2 1
6 6 6 2 3 2 2 5 3 3 2 4 4 4
6 3 3 1 3 5 1 5 5 5 2 6 6 4
6 3 2 2 5 5 3 2 2 6 6 6 6
4 4 4 4 3 1 5 3 3 1 3 3 3 1
3 2 3 1 3 3 2 5 6 6 6 6 6 6
3 2 3 4 4 4 2 5 5 5 3 4 1 4
3 1 3 4 2 2 1 6 5 3 3 4 2 4
5 5 5 5 6 6 6 6 2 1 1 4 2 4
5 4 2 2 5 1 6 1 2 3 5 3 3 4
4 4 5 5 5 6 2 2 3 3 5 5 3 1
4 6 5 1 3 6 6 6 4 5 5 4 4 4
6 6 6 6 3 6 3 6 4 4 2 2 5 5 4
4 4 4 6 6 3 3 4 5 1 4 1 5 5
4 3 3 5 1 3 2 5 5 5 5 4 4 5
5 3 5 5 3 3 2 1 2 1 2 2 4 1
5 2 5 1 5 5 3 5 2 5 3 5 2 2
5 2 5 3 5 1 3 5 5 5 3 5 5 5
5 5 3 3 5 5 3 2 2 1 3 2 2 5
```

HASHI

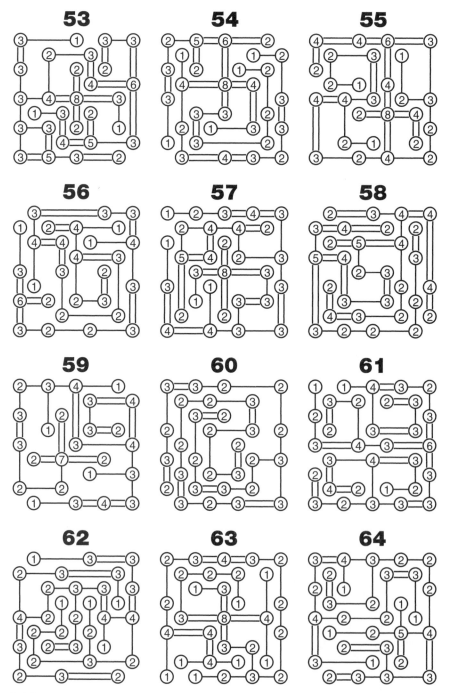

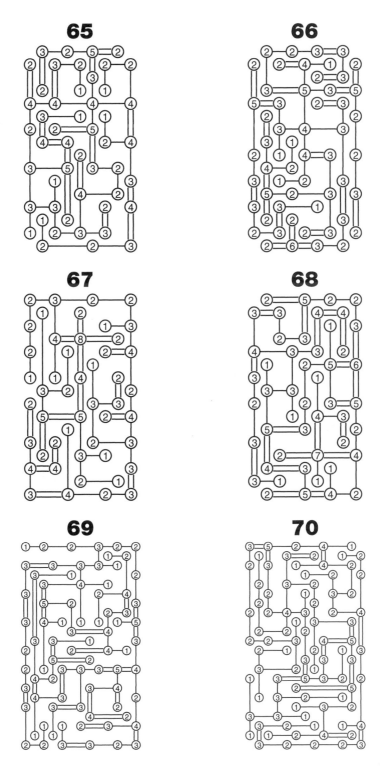

65

66

67

68

69

70

313

71

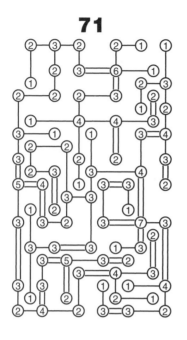

72

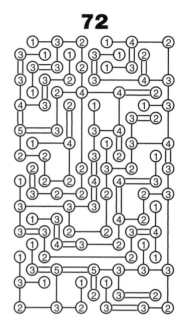

73

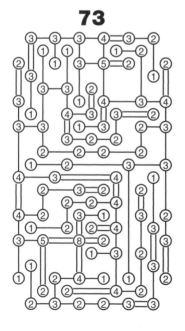

74

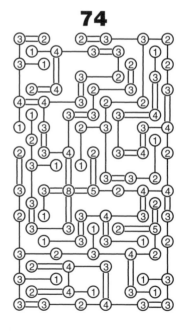

75

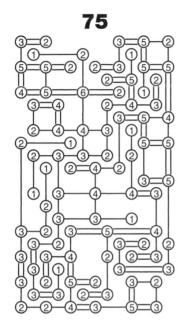

76

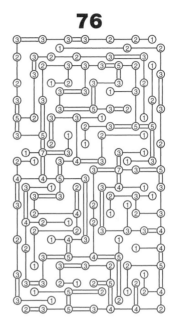

77

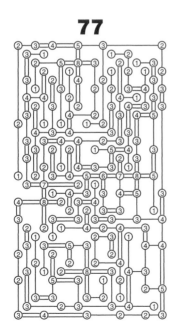

78

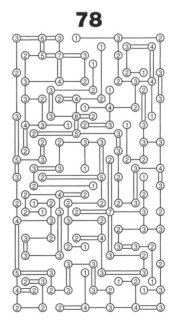

315

HEYAWAKE

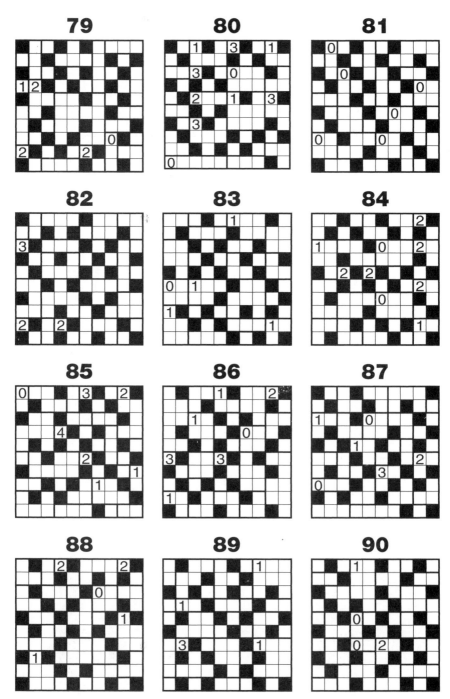

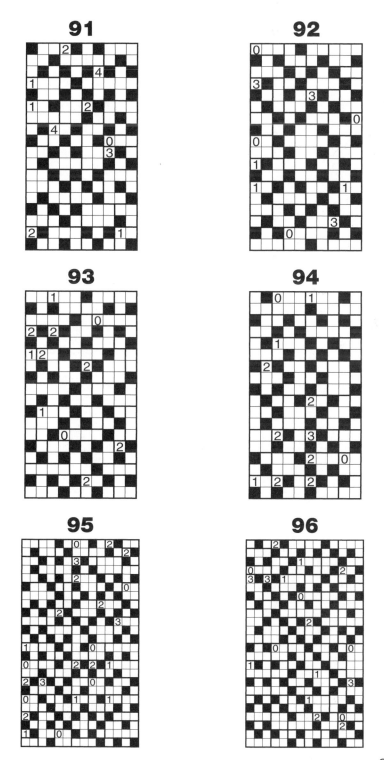

97

98

99

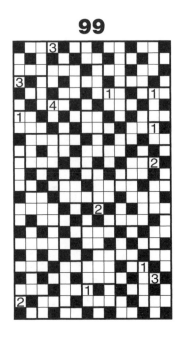

100

101

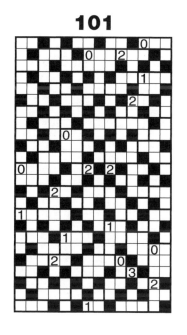

102

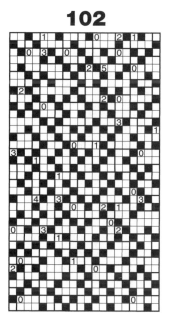

103

104

HITORI

105

	3		2	4		7	
5	1	8		2	3	6	4
	6	5	4	7	2	8	
4		2		3		1	7
3	2		6	8	1		5
7	5	3		1		2	6
	7		5		6		3
1	4	6	7	5	8	3	2

106

8	2	5		1		3	6
	4	8	2	3	5		7
6		7	1		8	2	3
5	3		8	2		7	
2		4	5		3		1
7	8	2		5	6	1	4
3	5	1	6		4		8
4		6	3	7	1	8	

107

5	3		1		8	2	
6		5	2	7		1	4
8	1		7		2	3	
1		7	4	5		6	8
3	4		6		7		2
4	2	6	3	8	1	5	7
	7	3	5	2		8	
7	6		8		3	4	5

108

	1	3	2		7	8	
2		4	8	3		1	5
3	4		7	6	2	5	
7		6		2		4	1
4	7	8	1	5	3	6	
5	6		4	1		3	2
	3	1		4	5		6
1	5	2	3		8	7	

109

	1	3		2	5	4	
1		4	6		3	2	8
2	4	5		7		3	
3		6	1	4	2	5	7
	2	7	5		8		6
4		2		8	7	6	
8	3	1	4		6	7	5
	5		7	6		8	

110

	2	1	3		4		6
1		6		2	8	7	3
8	1	2	6	5	7		4
3		8		1		2	5
5	3		4		2		7
4		7	2	8	3	5	
2	5		7		6	4	1
	8	4	5	7		3	

111

6		4	2	5	7	8	1
3	6		5		4		2
7	3	5	8	1		6	4
	2		6		3	4	5
4	5	7		3		2	
5	8	3	1	2	6		7
2		8		4		1	3
8	7		3	6	1	5	

112

	3		4		5	8	
5	6	1	7	8		4	2
	7	8	6		4	2	
8		5		2		1	3
1	2	3	8	6	7		4
	1	2		3		6	7
3	4		2	5	1		8
	8	6		4	2	3	1

113

6		5	8		4	3	
1	6	3		2	5		4
4		8	5	3	1	6	7
5	3		1		7		2
7		4		6	3	2	1
	1	6	7	5	2		3
8	2	7		4		5	
	4		2	7	6	1	5

114

6		8	7		3		1
2	4	3		6	1	7	5
	3		8		7		4
4	6	1	5	2		3	8
	1	4		3	8	2	7
3	5		1		4	6	
5		2	4	7	6	8	3
	7	5		4		1	

115

	1	2		4	6	7	
1		7	3		8		5
2	4		8	3	1	5	6
3	5	6		7		2	
	2	5	6		4	8	1
7		1		2	3		8
4	7	3	1	5	2	6	
	8		7	1		3	2

116

	6	5	8		7	4	1
7		1		2		3	
6	5	7	2	8	3	1	4
3	2		1		4	6	7
1		4	7	3		8	
	4	8	5		1	2	3
8	3	6		1	5	7	2
	8		6	4	2		5

117

118

119

120

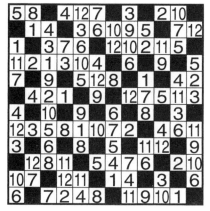

121

122

123

124

125

126

127

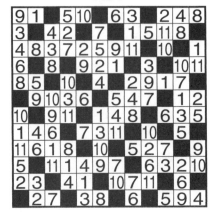

128

LITS

129

130

131

132

133

134

135

136

137

138

139

140

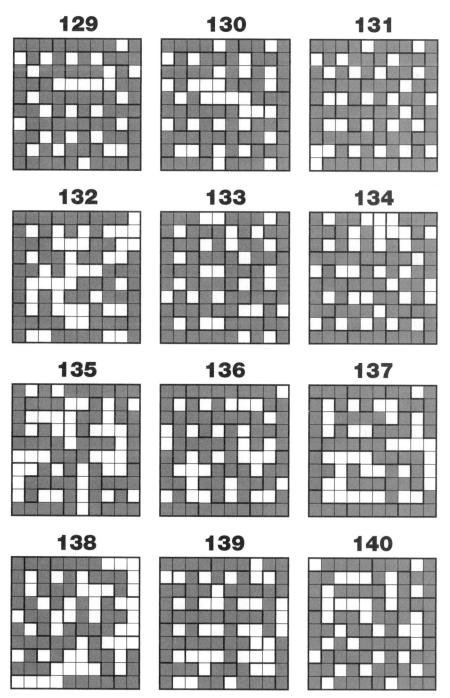

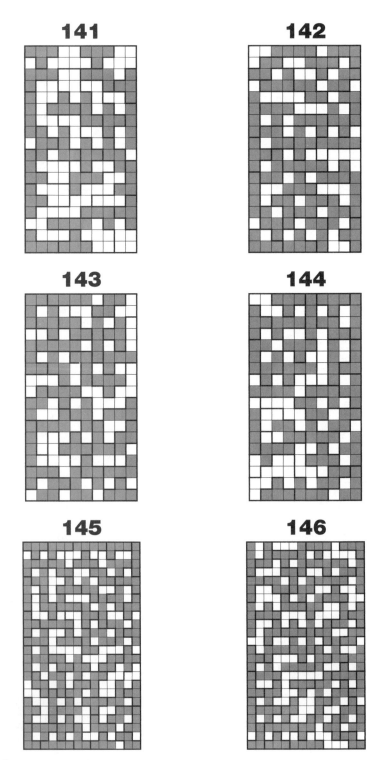

141 142
143 144
145 146

147

148

149

150

151

152

153

154

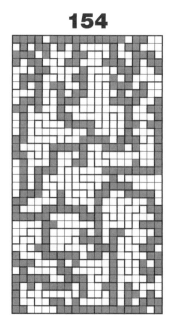

155

156

157

158

159

160

161

162

163

164

165

166

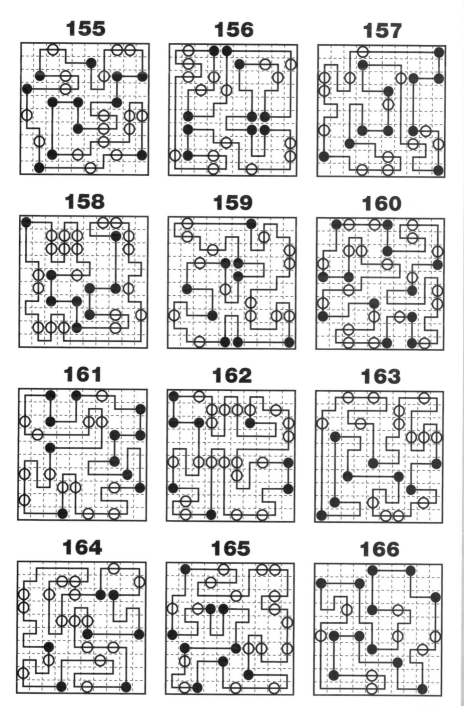

167

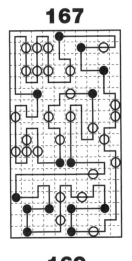

168

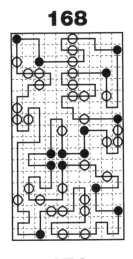

169

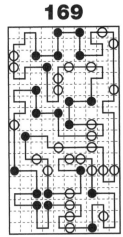

170

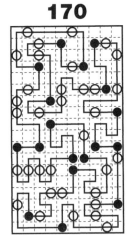

171

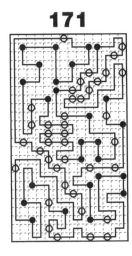

172

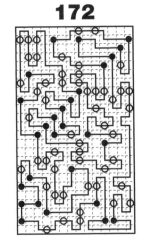

173

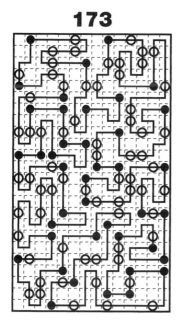

174

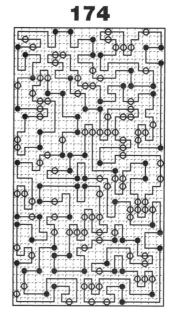

175

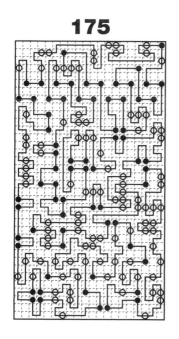

176

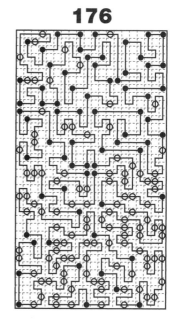

329

177

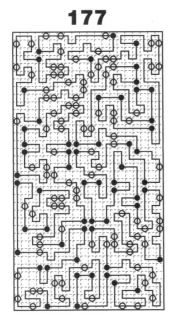

178

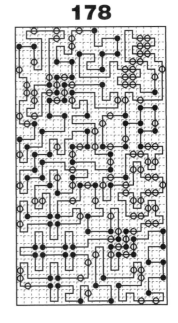

179

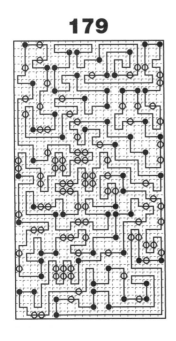

180

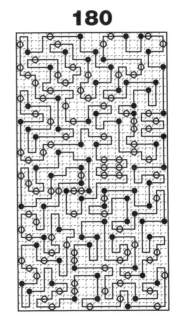

NUMBER LINK

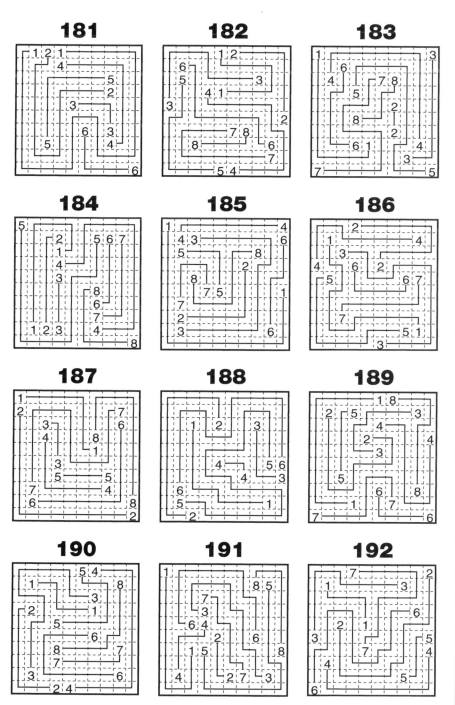

193

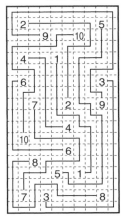

194

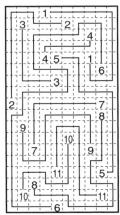

195

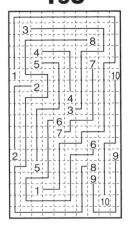

196

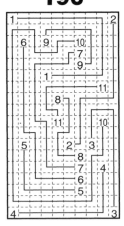

197

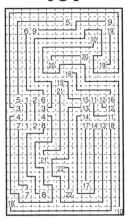

198

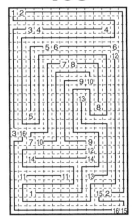

199

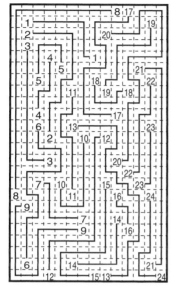

200

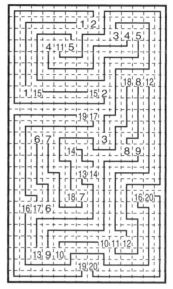

201

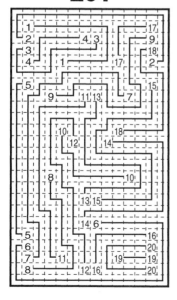

202

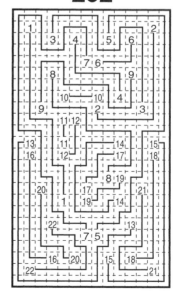

203

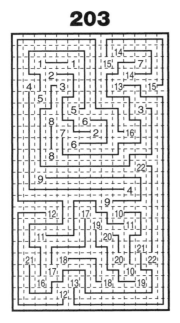

204

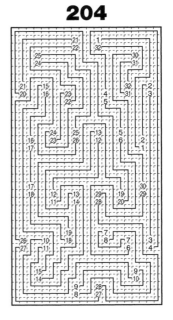

205

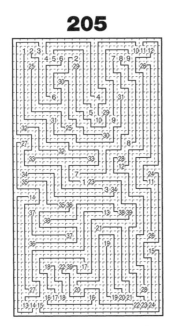

206

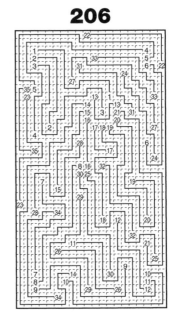

334

NURIKABE

219

220

221

222

223

224

225

226

227

228

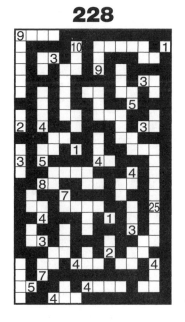

229

230

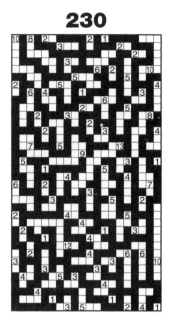

231

232

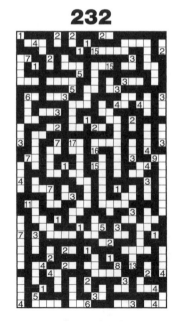

RIPPLE EFFECT

233

4	2	1	3	1	2	1	3
1	3	2	1	4	1	2	1
3	4	1	2	1	3	1	4
2	1	3	1	2	4	3	2
1	2	1	4	3	1	2	1
4	1	2	3	1	2	4	3
1	3	4	1	2	3	1	2
2	1	3	2	4	1	2	1

234

2	1	3	2	1	4	3	2
1	2	1	3	2	1	4	3
3	1	2	1	3	2	1	4
2	3	1	2	4	3	2	1
1	2	3	1	2	1	3	2
4	1	2	3	1	2	1	3
3	4	1	2	3	1	4	1
2	3	4	1	2	3	1	2

235

2	1	4	3	1	5	1	2
1	3	1	2	4	1	3	1
3	1	2	4	1	2	1	3
2	4	3	1	2	1	4	2
1	5	1	2	1	3	2	1
4	3	2	1	5	1	3	4
2	1	4	3	2	5	1	2
3	2	1	4	3	1	2	1

236

3	2	4	1	2	1	3	2
4	1	2	3	1	2	1	4
1	3	1	2	4	3	2	1
2	1	3	1	2	1	4	3
3	2	1	4	3	5	1	2
1	4	2	3	1	2	5	1
2	3	4	1	2	3	1	4
4	1	3	2	1	4	2	3

237

3	1	2	1	4	2	1	5
2	3	1	2	1	3	2	4
1	2	3	1	2	1	3	2
4	1	2	3	1	2	1	3
3	5	4	2	3	1	2	1
2	3	1	4	1	3	1	2
1	2	3	5	2	1	3	4
5	4	2	3	1	2	1	3

238

2	1	4	1	3	1	2	1
1	3	1	2	1	3	1	2
3	1	2	1	4	1	3	1
2	5	1	3	1	2	1	4
4	2	3	1	2	5	4	3
1	4	1	2	3	1	2	1
3	1	2	5	1	4	1	2
2	3	4	1	2	1	3	5

239

1	2	1	3	1	2	1	6
2	1	3	2	5	4	3	2
1	4	2	1	3	1	2	1
3	2	1	4	1	2	1	3
2	1	4	3	2	1	6	4
1	3	2	1	4	3	2	5
4	2	1	5	1	2	3	1
3	1	5	1	3	4	1	2

240

2	3	1	2	1	3	1	2
3	5	4	1	3	1	2	4
5	1	2	3	1	2	4	1
1	2	3	1	2	1	3	2
2	4	1	2	1	3	2	1
3	1	2	1	3	2	1	5
4	2	1	3	2	4	5	2
1	3	4	2	5	1	3	4

241

1	2	1	3	2	1	4	1
3	1	2	1	4	2	1	3
2	3	1	4	5	1	2	1
4	1	5	2	1	3	1	2
1	2	3	1	2	1	3	1
2	4	1	3	1	2	1	3
1	3	2	1	4	1	2	1
5	1	4	2	1	3	1	2

242

1	2	1	3	2	1	4	3
3	1	2	1	4	2	3	1
2	3	1	2	1	3	5	2
1	2	4	1	3	1	2	4
4	1	2	3	1	2	1	3
3	4	1	5	2	1	3	2
2	1	3	2	1	4	1	5
1	3	2	1	4	3	2	1

243

5	3	1	4	1	2	3	5
3	2	4	1	3	1	2	4
1	4	1	2	1	3	1	2
2	1	3	1	2	1	4	1
4	2	1	3	1	4	2	3
3	1	2	1	4	2	5	1
2	3	1	2	1	3	1	2
1	2	3	4	2	1	3	1

244

1	2	1	3	1	2	1	3
3	1	2	4	3	1	2	1
2	4	1	2	5	3	1	2
1	2	3	1	2	4	3	1
4	1	2	3	1	2	1	3
2	3	1	2	4	1	2	1
3	1	4	1	3	5	1	4
1	2	3	4	2	1	3	1

245

```
1 2 1 3 2 1 4 3 2 1
3 1 2 1 3 2 1 4 3 2
2 3 1 2 1 3 2 1 4 3
1 2 3 1 2 1 3 2 1 4
4 1 2 3 1 2 1 3 2 1
3 4 1 2 3 1 2 1 3 2
2 3 4 1 2 3 1 4 1 3
1 2 3 4 1 2 3 1 2 1
5 1 2 3 6 1 2 3 1 2
1 5 1 2 3 4 1 2 3 1
2 1 6 1 4 3 5 1 2 4
4 2 3 5 2 1 3 6 4 2
1 3 4 2 1 5 1 2 1 3
3 1 2 1 3 2 4 1 2 1
6 4 1 3 5 1 2 3 1 2
5 2 3 1 2 4 1 2 3 1
1 3 1 2 4 3 5 1 2 3
2 1 4 1 3 2 1 4 1 2
```

246

```
1 2 1 3 4 1 2 1 5 2
2 1 3 4 1 2 5 3 4 1
1 3 4 5 2 3 1 2 1 3
3 4 1 2 1 5 3 4 2 1
5 1 2 1 3 4 1 5 1 2
2 5 1 3 2 1 4 2 3 1
1 2 3 4 1 2 1 3 2 4
3 1 2 1 4 1 3 1 5 2
2 3 1 5 2 3 1 2 4 1
4 2 5 1 3 1 2 4 3 5
1 4 2 3 5 2 1 3 1 2
2 1 3 2 1 4 5 1 2 1
1 2 1 4 2 1 3 5 1 4
3 1 2 1 3 5 1 2 3 1
2 5 1 3 4 1 2 3 5 2
1 2 4 1 2 3 1 4 1 5
4 3 2 5 1 2 3 1 2 1
3 4 1 2 3 1 4 2 1 3
```

247

```
3 2 1 5 4 2 3 6 1 4
1 4 3 1 2 1 4 3 5 2
2 3 4 2 5 3 1 2 4 1
4 2 6 3 1 5 2 4 1 3
3 1 2 1 3 4 6 1 3 2
1 6 3 4 2 1 5 3 6 1
2 3 1 6 4 2 3 5 2 4
1 4 5 2 1 3 2 1 4 2
5 2 1 3 2 1 4 2 3 1
4 5 3 1 6 2 1 3 2 5
6 3 4 2 1 5 3 4 1 6
3 1 2 1 3 4 2 6 5 3
1 2 1 4 2 3 6 1 2 4
2 1 3 2 4 1 5 3 1 2
4 3 2 1 5 6 3 2 4 1
3 4 1 5 2 1 4 1 2 3
1 6 4 3 1 5 2 4 3 2
5 2 3 4 6 2 1 3 1 4
```

248

```
2 1 3 1 7 4 3 1 2 1
1 3 7 8 6 1 5 2 3 4
3 5 1 4 8 2 1 7 1 6
2 1 6 2 1 3 2 1 8 5
1 4 2 1 3 8 7 4 1 3
4 8 1 3 1 6 1 5 4 1
1 7 5 6 4 2 3 1 5 2
3 2 4 1 2 5 1 2 1 4
1 3 1 7 5 1 2 6 3 1
5 1 2 3 1 2 1 3 2 8
2 5 1 8 6 4 3 7 1 5
7 1 6 1 3 1 2 1 4 6
3 4 8 2 1 7 6 4 3 1
1 2 1 5 4 3 1 8 1 2
4 1 3 1 8 2 5 1 2 1
5 3 2 6 7 1 4 5 1 3
1 2 1 3 2 8 1 2 4 1
3 1 5 4 1 6 7 3 1 2
```

249

```
1 2 1 3 1 2 1 3 2 1
3 1 2 1 4 1 3 2 1 4
2 3 4 2 1 6 2 1 5 1
1 2 1 5 3 4 1 6 2 3
5 4 2 3 1 2 4 5 3 2
3 6 1 4 5 3 2 1 4 1
1 2 3 1 4 5 3 2 1 4
2 5 4 7 1 2 1 3 2 1
4 1 6 2 3 4 5 1 3 2
1 3 5 6 1 3 2 4 1 3
2 1 3 4 2 1 3 2 4 1
1 4 2 3 5 2 4 3 1 2
3 7 1 2 3 5 6 1 2 1
6 5 4 1 2 3 1 2 1 3
4 2 3 5 6 4 2 1 3 2
2 1 5 3 1 2 1 4 2 1
3 4 2 1 3 7 5 2 1 4
1 3 1 4 1 6 2 1 4 3
```

250

```
3 2 1 6 1 2 1 3 1 2
4 1 2 3 5 1 4 1 2 1
1 3 1 5 2 3 1 2 1 3
2 1 4 1 3 1 2 4 3 2
3 2 1 4 1 2 1 3 5 1
6 1 5 3 2 4 1 3 5 1
4 3 1 2 1 3 2 5 1 2
1 4 2 1 3 2 4 1 2 3
2 1 3 5 2 1 3 2 1 5
1 2 1 3 1 6 2 1 3 4
3 1 2 4 6 2 1 3 2 1
4 3 1 2 1 3 5 2 1 3
2 1 3 1 2 1 4 1 5 2
1 2 1 3 1 5 6 4 2 1
3 1 2 1 3 2 1 5 3 6
1 3 1 2 4 1 2 1 5 3
2 1 4 1 2 3 1 6 4 3
1 2 1 3 5 1 2 3 1 2
```

251

1	3	2	1	4	2	3	1	5	4
2	4	3	5	2	1	6	2	3	1
3	5	1	2	1	3	1	4	2	3
4	1	2	3	5	4	2	3	1	2
2	3	1	4	1	2	1	5	4	1
5	1	3	2	4	1	5	1	3	4
3	2	4	1	2	3	1	2	1	3
1	4	2	5	1	2	3	4	2	5
2	1	5	3	6	4	2	3	5	2
4	2	3	1	2	5	4	2	3	1
3	1	2	4	1	3	1	5	4	3
2	3	4	2	5	1	3	1	2	4
5	4	1	3	1	2	5	4	1	2
1	5	2	1	3	4	1	2	3	1
4	2	3	5	2	1	4	3	2	5
1	3	5	4	1	3	2	1	4	3
2	1	4	2	6	1	3	5	1	2
1	2	1	3	4	5	1	2	3	4

252

1	2	3	4	1	5	1	2	1	3
2	3	1	5	2	4	3	1	2	1
3	1	2	1	3	1	2	4	1	2
1	2	4	3	1	2	1	5	3	1
2	1	3	2	5	1	4	3	2	6
1	3	2	1	4	3	2	6	5	2
3	2	1	4	1	2	3	1	4	1
1	4	5	2	3	1	6	2	1	3
2	1	6	1	2	4	5	3	2	1
4	2	1	5	1	3	2	4	1	2
1	5	2	3	4	2	1	5	3	4
2	3	1	2	5	1	3	1	2	1
1	2	3	4	1	5	2	3	1	2
3	1	5	1	2	4	1	2	6	3
5	4	2	3	1	2	5	4	2	1
2	3	4	1	6	3	2	1	4	2
1	2	1	5	3	1	4	2	3	1
3	1	2	4	1	2	6	5	1	3

253

2	1	4	1	2	1	3	4	1	2
1	2	3	5	1	2	4	1	2	3
3	1	6	1	4	7	1	2	3	1
4	6	1	3	5	1	2	1	4	2
5	1	2	6	1	2	3	5	2	1
1	2	3	1	2	5	1	4	1	3
3	5	1	4	1	6	2	3	5	1
6	1	2	3	4	2	5	1	3	2
1	2	4	1	3	1	6	2	1	4
2	1	3	5	1	4	3	1	2	1
1	3	6	1	2	1	4	5	1	2
4	1	2	3	1	2	7	3	6	1
2	4	1	6	7	5	1	4	1	3
3	2	5	4	3	1	2	6	3	2
1	3	2	1	4	2	3	1	2	5
2	1	4	2	1	3	5	2	4	1
1	2	1	3	2	4	1	3	1	2
3	1	2	1	3	1	2	1	3	1

254

5	3	4	1	2	3	1	4	5	1
3	2	1	4	5	1	2	3	1	2
2	4	3	5	6	2	4	1	2	5
4	1	2	1	3	4	1	2	6	3
1	3	1	2	4	3	2	5	1	4
3	5	4	1	2	1	3	1	2	1
2	1	6	3	1	5	1	2	4	6
1	4	2	1	3	6	4	1	5	3
4	1	3	2	1	4	5	6	3	2
3	2	1	5	4	3	1	2	1	5
1	3	5	4	6	2	3	1	2	1
2	6	1	2	5	1	2	3	1	4
1	4	2	3	1	5	1	4	6	2
3	5	4	1	2	3	6	5	2	3
5	1	6	2	3	4	1	2	3	1
6	7	2	1	4	1	2	3	1	5
4	3	5	6	1	2	3	1	5	4
3	2	1	4	5	3	1	2	4	6

255

```
2 5 3 1 4 2 1 3 2 1
3 1 4 2 1 3 2 1 4 2
1 2 5 1 3 4 1 2 1 3
4 1 2 3 1 5 6 4 2 1
2 3 1 4 5 2 3 1 6 4
1 4 3 1 2 6 1 2 3 5
3 2 4 5 3 1 2 1 4 3
6 5 2 3 1 2 4 6 5 1
2 1 6 1 4 3 5 2 1 6
4 3 5 2 1 4 1 3 2 1
5 1 3 4 7 1 2 1 3 4
3 4 2 1 6 2 3 4 1 2
1 2 1 5 3 1 4 2 6 5
2 3 4 6 5 3 2 1 4 3
4 1 3 2 1 4 1 5 3 2
3 2 1 4 2 1 3 2 1 4
1 4 2 3 1 2 1 3 2 1
2 5 1 2 3 1 2 4 1 2
```

256

```
2 1 3 1 2 4 5 3 2 6 1 2 1 4
1 2 1 4 1 3 2 6 4 1 2 1 3 2
3 1 2 1 3 1 4 1 5 3 1 4 1 3
2 4 1 3 1 2 6 4 3 1 5 2 4 1
1 2 3 1 2 1 3 2 1 5 4 3 1 2
4 3 1 2 1 3 1 5 2 4 3 1 2 5
3 1 2 4 6 5 2 1 4 3 1 5 1 3
5 6 1 3 2 4 5 3 1 2 6 4 5 1
1 4 5 2 3 1 4 6 5 1 2 3 4 2
2 3 4 5 1 2 3 4 1 6 5 2 3 4
6 1 2 1 4 1 2 1 3 5 4 6 1 3
3 5 1 2 1 3 6 5 2 1 3 1 2 1
1 2 3 4 5 2 1 3 1 4 1 2 1 5
2 4 1 3 2 1 5 2 4 1 2 3 5 2
4 1 5 2 3 6 4 1 2 3 1 5 1 4
3 2 4 5 1 3 1 6 1 2 5 4 2 1
1 3 2 1 6 5 2 4 3 1 2 1 4 3
2 1 3 6 4 2 3 5 2 4 6 3 1 2
1 5 1 3 2 4 1 3 1 2 1 6 2 1
5 1 2 4 3 1 5 2 4 1 3 1 5 4
1 4 1 2 5 3 4 1 2 3 1 2 1 3
4 1 3 5 2 1 3 4 6 1 2 1 3 1
1 2 4 3 1 5 1 2 1 4 1 3 1 2
2 3 5 1 4 1 2 1 5 2 3 1 2 1
```

257

```
3 1 4 2 1 3 2 1 4 3 1 2 1 3
2 5 6 3 2 4 1 3 1 2 4 1 5 2
1 2 3 4 1 2 3 1 6 5 1 4 2 1
4 1 2 1 3 1 4 2 3 1 2 1 3 4
2 3 1 2 1 3 2 5 1 3 1 6 1 2
3 2 5 6 4 2 7 1 2 4 5 2 6 3
5 1 2 3 1 4 1 3 1 2 1 3 4 1
1 4 3 2 5 1 3 2 7 6 2 4 3 2
4 2 1 5 3 2 6 4 2 1 3 5 1 4
3 1 2 4 6 1 8 1 3 5 4 1 2 3
1 3 4 2 1 3 5 2 4 3 1 2 5 1
2 1 3 1 4 5 2 3 1 2 6 1 4 5
5 4 1 3 1 2 4 6 5 7 2 3 1 2
4 5 2 6 3 4 1 5 2 1 3 1 2 1
1 2 1 4 2 3 7 2 1 3 4 2 1 3
2 3 4 5 1 2 1 3 4 1 5 1 3 4
3 1 5 7 6 1 3 4 1 2 1 3 2 1
1 2 6 1 4 5 2 1 3 4 2 6 1 2
2 4 1 2 5 3 1 2 1 3 1 2 4 3
1 5 3 4 1 2 6 1 2 1 3 5 2 1
3 1 4 1 3 6 1 5 1 2 4 1 3 2
2 3 1 2 1 7 2 4 3 6 1 2 5 4
4 2 5 3 2 4 1 3 2 1 5 4 1 3
1 6 3 1 4 1 3 2 1 4 3 1 2 1
```

258

```
2 1 3 2 1 4 1 3 1 2 1 3 2 1
1 2 1 5 2 3 4 1 2 1 3 2 1 4
3 1 2 1 3 6 5 2 1 3 4 1 5 3
2 4 1 3 5 1 2 1 3 1 2 5 3 2
1 2 5 4 1 2 1 3 2 4 5 2 1 6
4 1 3 1 2 1 6 1 4 1 3 1 2 1
2 3 1 2 1 3 4 6 5 3 1 4 1 3
3 2 4 1 6 5 1 2 1 7 4 2 3 1
1 4 2 3 1 7 2 3 6 1 2 3 4 2
5 1 3 2 4 1 3 5 2 4 3 1 2 1
2 3 1 4 2 3 1 2 1 5 1 2 1 3
3 1 2 1 3 1 2 1 4 6 5 1 3 4
4 5 1 2 1 4 1 3 5 1 4 3 1 2
2 1 4 1 2 5 3 6 1 2 3 1 2 5
1 2 3 5 1 6 4 2 3 1 2 4 6 1
3 4 1 2 3 1 5 4 2 3 6 1 5 2
5 1 2 3 4 2 1 5 1 4 1 2 3 1
1 2 1 4 5 1 3 1 4 2 3 5 1 4
2 1 5 2 1 3 1 2 1 5 2 3 4 2
1 5 3 1 2 1 4 3 2 1 5 1 2 1
4 2 1 3 1 2 1 4 1 3 1 2 1 3
1 6 2 5 3 4 2 1 3 2 4 1 3 1
2 1 4 1 2 1 3 2 4 1 2 3 1 2
1 3 1 2 4 3 5 1 2 4 3 1 2 1
```

342

SHIKAKU

259

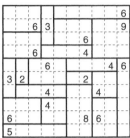

260

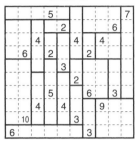

261

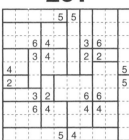

262

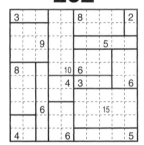

263

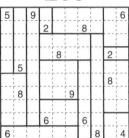

264

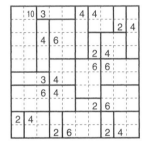

265

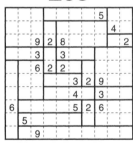

266

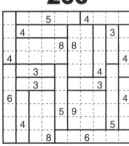

267

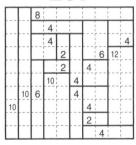

268

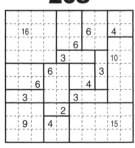

269

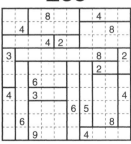

270

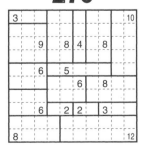

271

272

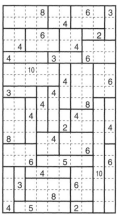

273

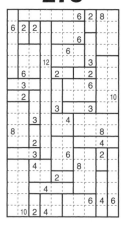

274

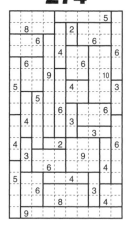

275

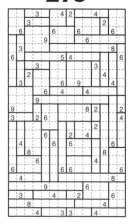

276

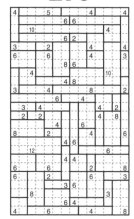

344

277

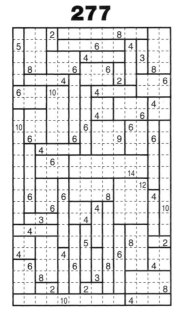

278

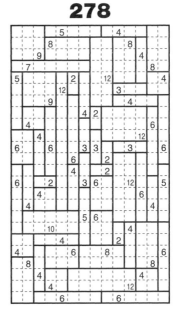

279

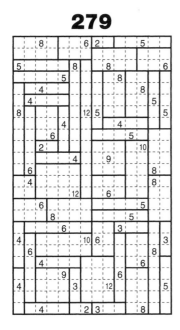

280

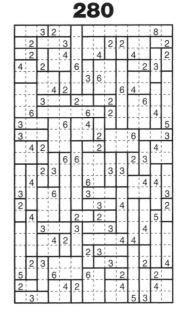

281

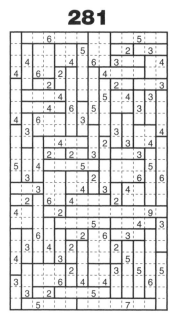

282

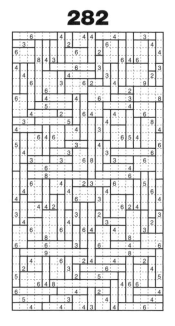

283

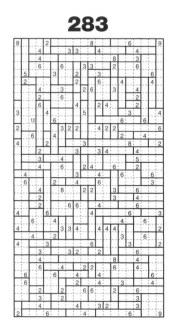

284

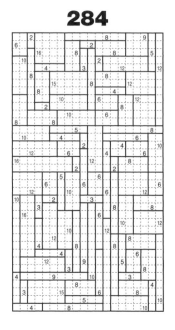

SLITHERLINK

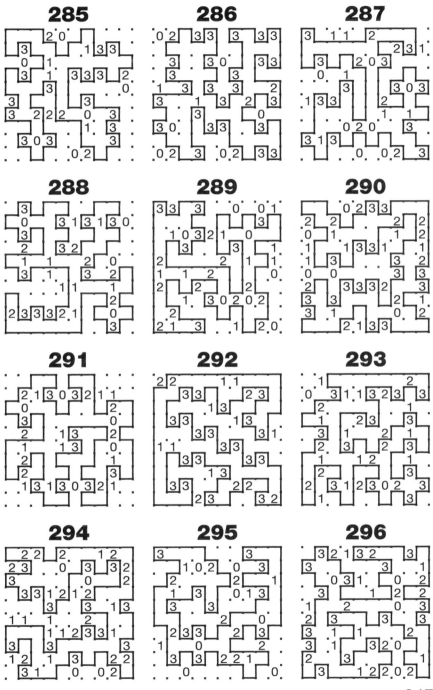

297

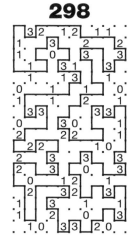

298

299

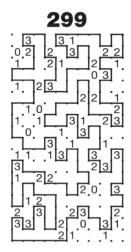

300

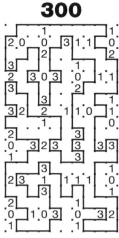

301

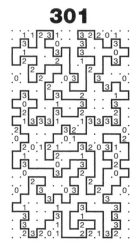

302

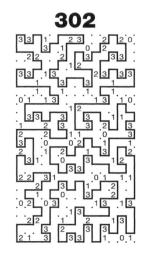

303

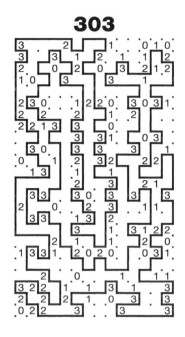

304

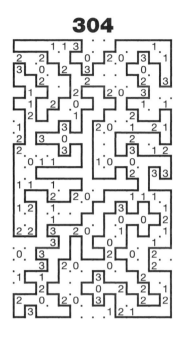

305

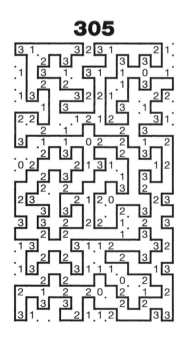

306

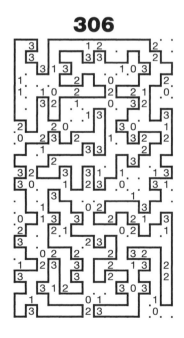

307

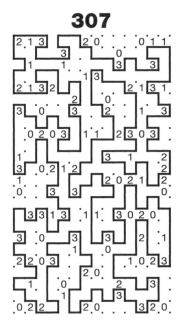

308

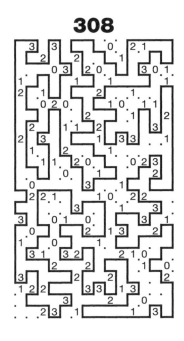

309

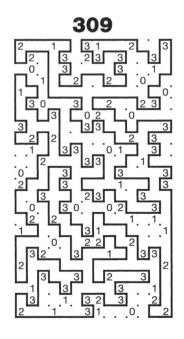

310

YAJILIN

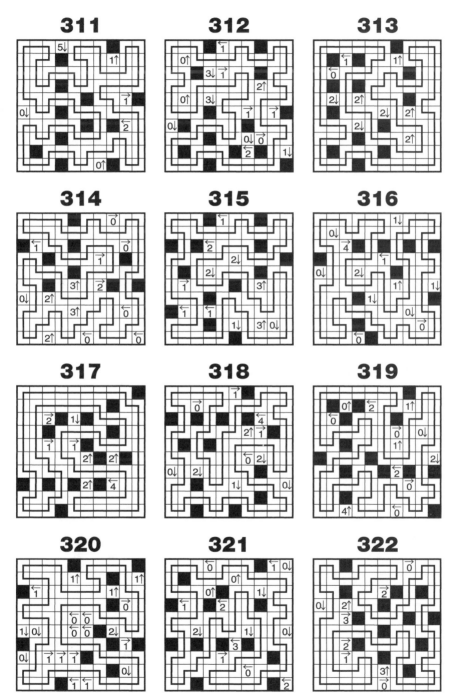

323

324

325

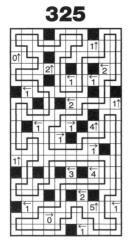

326

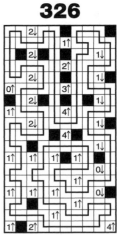

327

328

352

329

330

331

332

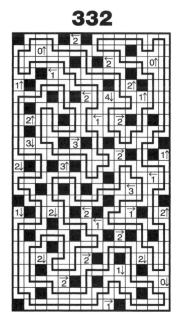

353

333

334

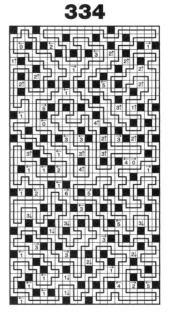

335

336

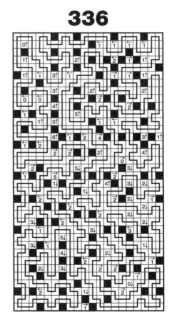

SUDOKU

337

```
6 3 8 9 2 5 1 4 7
9 1 4 7 3 8 2 5 6
7 5 2 1 4 6 9 8 3
2 4 3 5 6 7 8 9 1
5 8 7 2 1 9 6 3 4
1 9 6 3 8 4 5 7 2
8 7 1 4 9 2 3 6 5
4 2 9 6 5 3 7 1 8
3 6 5 8 7 1 4 2 9
```

338

```
7 8 6 2 1 4 9 3 5
9 2 4 5 8 3 7 6 1
5 1 3 9 6 7 4 8 2
6 9 2 4 5 8 3 1 7
8 4 5 7 3 1 6 2 9
3 7 1 6 9 2 5 4 8
2 6 9 1 4 5 8 7 3
1 5 8 3 7 6 2 9 4
4 3 7 8 2 9 1 5 6
```

339

```
3 9 2 7 6 4 5 8 1
1 5 6 8 9 3 2 4 7
7 4 8 2 1 5 6 3 9
8 2 7 1 4 9 3 5 6
6 3 9 5 2 7 8 1 4
4 1 5 6 3 8 7 9 2
2 6 4 3 8 1 9 7 5
9 7 3 4 5 2 1 6 8
5 8 1 9 7 6 4 2 3
```

340

```
7 6 4 5 2 1 3 8 9
1 5 2 3 9 8 7 4 6
3 8 9 4 6 7 5 2 1
2 3 1 8 7 4 6 9 5
6 4 5 2 1 9 8 7 3
8 9 7 6 3 5 2 1 4
4 7 3 1 8 6 9 5 2
5 2 8 9 4 3 1 6 7
9 1 6 7 5 2 4 3 8
```

341

```
9 1 7 6 3 5 4 2 8
2 8 6 1 4 7 9 3 5
5 4 3 9 2 8 6 7 1
8 9 5 4 1 3 2 6 7
4 7 2 8 9 6 5 1 3
3 6 1 5 7 2 8 4 9
1 5 4 7 6 9 3 8 2
7 2 9 3 8 4 1 5 6
6 3 8 2 5 1 7 9 4
```

342

```
6 1 2 4 9 8 7 3 5
8 5 3 2 6 7 4 9 1
7 4 9 1 3 5 6 8 2
1 9 8 6 5 3 2 7 4
5 6 7 8 2 4 3 1 9
2 3 4 9 7 1 5 6 8
9 2 1 7 4 6 8 5 3
4 7 5 3 8 9 1 2 6
3 8 6 5 1 2 9 4 7
```

343

```
2 6 1 8 5 4 7 9 3
9 3 7 6 1 2 8 4 5
5 8 4 3 7 9 2 1 6
7 2 3 4 9 6 1 5 8
8 5 9 2 3 1 4 6 7
1 4 6 5 8 7 9 3 2
6 1 5 9 2 8 3 7 4
3 7 2 1 4 5 6 8 9
4 9 8 7 6 3 5 2 1
```

344

```
4 9 8 7 1 6 3 5 2
1 5 6 9 2 3 4 7 8
2 3 7 8 4 5 9 6 1
3 4 1 6 8 9 7 2 5
5 6 9 2 7 4 1 8 3
8 7 2 3 5 1 6 9 4
6 8 5 1 3 7 2 4 9
9 1 4 5 6 2 8 3 7
7 2 3 4 9 8 5 1 6
```

345

```
2 1 9 7 8 6 5 4 3
3 8 5 2 9 4 1 6 7
6 4 7 1 3 5 9 8 2
4 9 1 8 7 2 3 5 6
8 3 6 4 5 1 7 2 9
5 7 2 3 6 9 4 1 8
9 5 4 6 2 7 8 3 1
1 2 8 9 4 3 6 7 5
7 6 3 5 1 8 2 9 4
```

346

```
5 2 7 6 4 9 8 1 3
8 9 4 3 1 2 6 7 5
3 1 6 7 5 8 2 4 9
2 8 1 5 6 3 4 9 7
7 3 9 1 2 4 5 6 8
4 6 5 8 9 7 1 3 2
1 7 2 4 3 5 9 8 6
9 4 3 2 8 6 7 5 1
6 5 8 9 7 1 3 2 4
```

347

```
3 6 2 4 9 7 5 8 1
7 5 1 8 3 2 9 6 4
4 8 9 6 5 1 3 2 7
1 2 8 3 7 4 6 5 9
6 7 5 2 8 9 4 1 3
9 3 4 5 1 6 2 7 8
8 9 3 7 6 5 1 4 2
2 1 6 9 4 8 7 3 5
5 4 7 1 2 3 8 9 6
```

348

```
7 9 1 6 8 4 5 3 2
8 5 4 7 2 3 1 9 6
3 6 2 5 1 9 4 8 7
6 2 3 1 4 8 9 7 5
1 4 7 9 5 6 3 2 8
9 8 5 3 7 2 6 4 1
4 1 9 2 6 7 8 5 3
5 7 8 4 3 1 2 6 9
2 3 6 8 9 5 7 1 4
```

349

5	1	2	3	6	8	7	9	4
9	6	4	1	7	5	3	8	2
7	3	8	9	2	4	6	5	1
2	9	1	5	4	6	8	7	3
8	5	6	7	3	2	1	4	9
3	4	7	8	9	1	2	6	5
6	2	5	4	1	7	9	3	8
1	8	3	6	5	9	4	2	7
4	7	9	2	8	3	5	1	6

350

3	4	5	1	7	8	9	2	6
2	7	1	6	3	9	4	5	8
9	6	8	4	2	5	1	7	3
6	2	9	7	8	3	5	1	4
4	1	3	5	9	6	7	8	2
8	5	7	2	4	1	3	6	9
1	8	4	9	6	7	2	3	5
7	9	6	3	5	2	8	4	1
5	3	2	8	1	4	6	9	7

351

7	4	6	2	9	1	8	3	5
1	5	9	3	8	7	6	4	2
2	3	8	5	6	4	9	1	7
5	9	7	4	2	8	3	6	1
8	1	2	6	3	5	4	7	9
3	6	4	1	7	9	2	5	8
4	2	5	9	1	6	7	8	3
9	8	1	7	4	3	5	2	6
6	7	3	8	5	2	1	9	4

352

6	8	2	3	9	7	4	5	1
5	1	7	6	4	2	3	9	8
9	3	4	1	8	5	6	2	7
8	4	5	7	6	1	2	3	9
7	9	3	5	2	8	1	6	4
2	6	1	9	3	4	7	8	5
1	5	8	2	7	3	9	4	6
4	2	9	8	1	6	5	7	3
3	7	6	4	5	9	8	1	2

353

5	2	1	6	9	8	4	3	7
7	9	3	1	4	5	6	8	2
8	6	4	7	2	3	9	5	1
3	7	2	5	6	4	8	1	9
4	5	6	8	1	9	7	2	3
1	8	9	3	7	2	5	6	4
6	1	8	4	3	7	2	9	5
9	3	7	2	5	6	1	4	8
2	4	5	9	8	1	3	7	6

354

8	9	1	7	2	6	3	5	4
3	2	7	4	5	9	1	6	8
5	6	4	3	1	8	9	7	2
9	8	6	1	3	2	5	4	7
1	4	5	6	8	7	2	3	9
2	7	3	5	9	4	6	8	1
7	3	9	2	4	5	8	1	6
4	5	8	9	6	1	7	2	3
6	1	2	8	7	3	4	9	5

355

1	9	7	3	8	2	4	6	5
4	2	8	6	5	1	9	7	3
6	3	5	7	9	4	1	2	8
8	7	1	2	6	9	5	3	4
9	5	3	1	4	7	6	8	2
2	4	6	5	3	8	7	9	1
3	1	9	8	7	5	2	4	6
7	6	2	4	1	3	8	5	9
5	8	4	9	2	6	3	1	7

356

4	8	2	5	3	1	9	6	7
6	9	5	7	2	4	1	3	8
1	7	3	6	9	8	2	5	4
3	2	8	9	4	6	5	7	1
5	6	7	2	1	3	4	8	9
9	1	4	8	7	5	3	2	6
7	3	6	1	5	9	8	4	2
8	5	1	4	6	2	7	9	3
2	4	9	3	8	7	6	1	5

357

4	2	3	1	9	7	6	5	8
1	5	7	3	8	6	2	9	4
9	8	6	4	5	2	7	1	3
6	4	1	2	3	5	9	8	7
5	7	8	9	1	4	3	6	2
2	3	9	7	6	8	5	4	1
7	6	5	8	4	3	1	2	9
8	1	2	5	7	9	4	3	6
3	9	4	6	2	1	8	7	5

358

5	4	9	6	7	3	1	2	8
7	1	3	8	2	5	9	4	6
8	2	6	4	1	9	5	7	3
1	3	8	2	9	4	7	6	5
4	5	2	1	6	7	8	3	9
6	9	7	3	5	8	4	1	2
3	7	4	5	8	6	2	9	1
9	8	1	7	3	2	6	5	4
2	6	5	9	4	1	3	8	7

359

3	8	7	1	5	2	9	6	4
1	4	9	8	6	3	5	7	2
6	2	5	9	7	4	8	3	1
8	7	3	6	2	9	4	1	5
4	1	2	3	8	5	6	9	7
9	5	6	7	4	1	2	8	3
2	6	8	5	1	7	3	4	9
7	9	4	2	3	8	1	5	6
5	3	1	4	9	6	7	2	8

360

4	7	6	9	5	3	2	8	1
8	2	5	7	6	1	3	9	4
9	3	1	2	8	4	7	5	6
6	9	7	3	4	2	5	1	8
1	8	4	5	9	7	6	2	3
2	5	3	8	1	6	4	7	9
3	4	8	1	7	5	9	6	2
7	1	2	6	3	9	8	4	5
5	6	9	4	2	8	1	3	7